Leading Inclusion in a Secondary School

Leading Inclusion in a Secondary School is a practical guide to one of the most challenging and rewarding roles in a secondary setting. It highlights the key responsibilities and offers practical advice on how to lead groups of staff, embed an ethos and, most importantly, be the advocate for all the children in the school.

Focusing on the core areas of inclusion – behaviour, SEND, safeguarding, attendance, pupil premium and OFSTED – the book provides an overview of each area and explores the skills and knowledge that are required to lead it successfully. Each chapter shares tried and tested strategies and systems for promoting inclusion alongside practical examples, case studies, thinking points and scenarios to take the reader on a comprehensive journey of the role.

This is an essential text for all current and aspiring leaders of inclusion including heads of year, senior leaders, safeguarding leads, welfare managers and so on, that will help to build an overarching strategy for inclusion in their school.

Mark Allen is the Principal of Trinity Academy St Edward's, part of the Trinity Multi-Academy Trust. He has over ten years' experience as a senior leader with a wealth of experience leading inclusion, safeguarding, HR and system leadership in secondary settings.

Leading Inclusion in a Secondary School

No Pupil Left Behind

Mark Allen

LONDON AND NEW YORK

First published 2022
by Routledge
2 Park Square, Milton Park, Abingdon, Oxon OX14 4RN

and by Routledge
52 Vanderbilt Avenue, New York, NY 10017

Routledge is an imprint of the Taylor & Francis Group, an informa business

© 2022 Mark Allen

The right of Mark Allen to be identified as author of this work has been asserted by him in accordance with sections 77 and 78 of the Copyright, Designs and Patents Act 1988.

All rights reserved. No part of this book may be reprinted or reproduced or utilised in any form or by any electronic, mechanical, or other means, now known or hereafter invented, including photocopying and recording, or in any information storage or retrieval system, without permission in writing from the publishers.

Trademark notice: Product or corporate names may be trademarks or registered trademarks, and are used only for identification and explanation without intent to infringe.

British Library Cataloguing-in-Publication Data
A catalogue record for this book is available from the British Library

Library of Congress Cataloging-in-Publication Data
Names: Allen, Mark, 1978– author.
Title: Leading inclusion in a secondary school : no pupil left behind / Mark Allen.
Description: Abingdon, Oxon ; New York, NY : Routledge, 2022.
Identifiers: LCCN 2021003671 | ISBN 9780367692162 (hardback) | ISBN 9780367692179 (paperback) | ISBN 9781003140924 (ebook)
Subjects: LCSH: Inclusive education. | Education, Secondary—Aims and objectives. | Educational leadership.
Classification: LCC LC1200 .A58 2022 | DDC 371.9/046—dc23
LC record available at https://lccn.loc.gov/2021003671

ISBN: 978-0-367-69216-2 (hbk)
ISBN: 978-0-367-69217-9 (pbk)
ISBN: 978-1-003-14092-4 (ebk)

Typeset in Melior
by Apex CoVantage, LLC

Contents

Acknowledgements — vi

Introduction: inclusion — 1

1 Developing an ethos — 3

2 Leadership – leading the line — 10

3 SEND and supporting your SENDCO — 30

4 Systems, systems, systems: developing, embedding and measuring — 48

5 Safeguarding — 75

6 Attendance — 93

7 Pupil premium — 107

8 Alternative provision — 121

9 The children — 132

10 OFSTED — 143

Glossary of terms — 148

Index — 150

Acknowledgements

The work in the pages that follow is not all mine. I have got to where I am due to working with exceptional people and being part of exceptional teams. To all my current and ex-colleagues, thank you for your trust, your time and your dedication. You really are superb professionals and I hope you take pride from seeing your ideas in this book.

A special thank you to the people who impacted my career the most:

Thanks to Neil O'Connor, Craig Parkinson and Damian Juriansz. You were excellent role models and your manner, excellent teaching and drive made me want to be like you.

Thanks to Helen Storey, Chas Ponsford and Mike Pollard. You gave me a chance, believed in me and started me on this leadership journey.

Thanks to Chris Robinson and Joanne Wilson. You empowered me, pushed me and showed me how to make positive change.

Final thanks go to Annamarie at Routledge, for always believing in this book and its importance, and to Molly at Routledge, who has been so helpful throughout the process.

To every single member of every team I have led, thank you for your belief, your effort and your unwavering determination to do the best for children.

Finally, and most importantly, thank you to my family for their unrelenting love, support and encouragement.

Mark

Introduction

Inclusion

The word 'inclusion' has become synonymous with education, but what does it actually mean? This book is about how a modern-day leader in a secondary setting can lead all the different aspects that incorporate inclusion. This book will give key insights into leading these different aspects and offer practical solutions to aid the reader's leadership of them.

What is inclusion?

> The term inclusion captures, in one word, an all-embracing societal ideology. Regarding individuals with disabilities and special education, inclusion secures opportunities for students with disabilities to learn alongside their non-disabled peers in general education classrooms.[1]

This book will touch on aspects of inclusion from a SEND perspective. Alongside this it will highlight the other key facets that make up inclusion as a whole. My experience of leading inclusion in a secondary school, or any educational setting, is that inclusion is much more than just SEND. SEND is a crucial area of inclusion, it helps to identify need and it gives us a framework to support our most vulnerable learners. A modern-day inclusion leader has to harness this and the other key areas to ensure that the school is truly inclusive.

These other key facets of inclusion are:

- Attendance
- Behaviour
- Safeguarding
- Pupil premium
- Systems and processes
- Alternative provision and more

Inclusion is about developing a child's knowledge, character and experiences to prepare them for what the world will throw at them. If you lead inclusion or 'pastoral' in a school setting I know you will understand my stance and hope you will find this book a useful and practical guide to leading all areas of inclusion well.

The book will give you an insight into the key areas of inclusion and it will give advice on how to lead them effectively. Each chapter will offer you an insight into my experiences and also offer the chance for you to reflect on yourself, your current setting and to start to formulate ideas you may have to improve things. Each chapter will end with a scenario for you to reflect on and think how you may solve it as a leader of inclusion. The detail in each chapter will provide you with the concept and the strategic and operational examples.

I have included lots of examples of strategies and initiatives that I or members of my teams have created over the years. I know these will be useful to you in your current role. Lots of professionals aspire to be a pastoral leader, and the aim of this book is to give you an insight into it and give you the confidence to take the role on. You may be a form tutor, a head of year, an associate head of year or a current senior leader. Whatever your role or experience this book will give you an idea of how to lead the area of inclusion successfully.

I hope my journey and my ideas can influence you and when times are hard in this very demanding profession to remember what we are really here for: **the children**.

Note

1 www.specialeducationguide.com/pre-k-12/inclusion

Developing an ethos

This chapter will focus on one of the most important components to a successful school. As a leader of education, it is vital that you develop an ethos in your school. This ethos should be entwined in everything that the staff and pupils do each day. An ethos sets the culture of the school, and a culture can be what either makes or breaks a school. This chapter will explore what an ethos and culture can be, and it gives an insight into what my ethos is. There is reference to my core values and discussion points about why each value is important and how they can help to set a culture. This chapter's scenario is about creating a new set of core values for a school and how you would go about doing that.

Introduction

Developing an ethos is the simplest thing to start your leadership journey on, but it is the one that gets missed too often. No matter what kind of leader you are, or what kind of school you work in, your ethos is pivotal to shaping you, your work and your impact. When I reflect as a leader, I can see how the ethos in some schools has changed over time. This can be due to a change of head teacher or as part of a new Multi-Academy Trust working with the school.

One of the biggest influences on the ethos of a school has been OFSTED and the increased accountability on leaders in schools. Too many leaders have been influenced by these pressures. It is important that from the outset you set your ethos, and this will drive the culture of your setting. If you get your ethos and your culture right then the environment for adults to work and children to learn will be created, and the rest will take care of itself and help to alleviate some of the external pressures.

> Your ethos as a leader will determine who you are and how you lead.
> Do not veer away from this.
> You are you, and your ethos has got you to where you are.

Shifting educational landscapes, external agencies, accountability measures and other leaders may all challenge this – be strong and be true to yourself and who you are.

What is an ethos?

A quick Google search gives us this definition:

> the fundamental character or spirit of a culture; the underlying sentiment that informs the beliefs, customs, or practices of a group or society; dominant assumptions of a people or period.
> the character or disposition of a community, group, person, etc.
> the moral element in dramatic literature that determines a character's action rather than his or her thought or emotion.

What this means for a school is that there should be an underlying current of this ethos in everything that goes on day by day. You should be able to see the ethos through staff/pupil interaction, through visual displays, through successes of the school and in every classroom. You can immediately get a feel for a school and for a classroom environment the moment you walk in. When you walk in a school that has a strong ethos it is almost tactile, and you get the sense of it as you speak to people and walk around.

Every single school that I have worked in had their own ethos. This may be a mission statement, or a group of key values or even as prescriptive a set of behaviours that determine who they are. When applying to work and to lead at a school, research their ethos and see if it aligns with yours.

Creating the ethos

So, who creates the ethos of a school? The head teacher most certainly should be part of it and usually is. The trust or academy chain will have a direct say on the ethos too. The most important people who should form part of the ethos of the school are the children. How many schools that you have worked in have had an ethos that is built around the children?

Why I am focusing on this? Simply put – children are my ethos. If you are to lead inclusion in a school, they have to be. As indicated in the earlier quote, there are key areas to focus that ethos on.

Fundamental character

To lead inclusion, you need a fundamental character. That character is a belief and a drive that you will do all you can do for all the children in the school.

Serving a community

An ethos needs to be driven and to be at the very heart of a community. As a leader of inclusion, you have to drive the same belief through every member of the community you serve.

Morality

The morals you possess as a leader will shape you. You must always maintain a clear moral purpose in all you do. As a leader of inclusion, that moral purpose should be to ensure children in your care are happy, and that they succeed and flourish.

Establishing an ethos – within the school and within your team

When you work in a school with challenging circumstances your ethos is what holds you and your work together. It is tested on a daily basis and it will be challenged by all. There are times when you make decisions that can appear to go against your ethos. You must remember that sometimes the decisions you make you will be plagued by, but they are made for the greater good of the community and for the greater good of the children in your care. As we go through the book you will see where decisions around exclusions, managed moves, attendance fines, SEN referrals, social care referrals and other sanctions can challenge your ethos and directly conflict what you set out to do.

This is the balance you have to create as a leader of inclusion, and these are the leadership challenges that you will face on a daily basis. If you can make those decisions where your morals and your fundamental beliefs are intertwined and that your community will benefit from, then it is a correct decision. People may challenge these decisions, and people will challenge you as a leader; remember to be true to your ethos.

Building a team ethos

When you take up a new post, part of your early work will be to establish your ethos with the staff and with the team you work with. From minute one you must communicate your ethos to your team and to the wider community. Don't be afraid to explain why you believe in your ethos and to explain to pupils and staff the reasoning behind it.

In the early days of your role you must adopt a leadership style that embodies your ethos, and you must spend time modelling the behaviour and promoting what you believe in at every opportunity. You will have situations where you have to challenge pupils and staff as their responses may not align to what you want. It is important you do this so that they see you mean business and that your ethos drives your work.

Work closely with your team. Their behaviour, their interactions and their work will reflect you as their leader and it will reflect your ethos. You have to make sure everyone is on the same page and consistently delivering your message. You should look to over-communicate your ethos in the early stages of establishing it. Over-communicate to your team by using daily briefings and structured meetings to ensure the ethos is always a standing item. Use formal procedures such as the development plan and appraisal to highlight the importance of the ethos. Everyone should be able to communicate the ethos verbally and through their daily actions. Make sure the children understand the ethos. Lead assemblies weekly, use tutor time and personal, social and health education (PSHE) and communicate it to parents and careers via letters, blogs and the school website. The more you deliver the message, the more it will become common practice.

My ethos

What follows is a statement that surmises my ethos and what I hold true to in every decision I make. I have always held children at the forefront of all I do: a leader of inclusion should. I watched the late Rita Pierson's TED Talk, and this has always resonated with me. If you haven't already, I would strongly recommend you watch it (www.ted.com/talks/rita_pierson_every_kid_needs_a_champion?language=en):

> Every child deserves a champion. An adult who will never give up on them, who understands the power of connection and insists they become the best that they can possibly be.

What this means in practice is that there are times when, as a leader of inclusion, you have to show that you support the child and their needs. Incidents of poor behaviour will happen on a daily basis, and the easiest decision in the world is to put a consequence in place without thought.

It is your job as a leader and as champion of children to make brave decisions that are in the best interest of the child. From time to time you will have difficult conversations about this. A school is open for its children; some of them face difficulties and haven't got an adult at home who can support them. A leader of inclusion needs to be that adult.

Colleagues may want a more severe consequence for an incident, but it is your duty to reflect on the situation and the needs of the child before making that decision. You must talk this through with the child and the adult. Never undermine a colleague in front of a child, however. You must ensure that the decision you make is in the best interest of that child.

Once your ethos is established, these decisions and conversations become easier and less frequent. Why? As interactions with staff and children become more positive, pupils' needs are met more regularly, and your ethos and culture become widespread in the classroom and wider school environment.

The ethos of a school and its leaders will determine how that school functions and how children will be supported within it. All the adults in the school should subscribe to the ethos, and the combination of the behaviours and ethos of those adults sets the culture of the school.

What is a culture?

The culture of a school is determined by its leaders. They set the tone, they set the working culture of their staff and they set the parameters of what is and isn't acceptable. It is a group of beliefs, attitudes, perceptions and rules that underpin all the school does.

The culture of a school has to be about the children. Schools can develop a culture that is the opposite to this: they function purely for the staff. Decisions are made that are for purely staff benefit rather than the children. A leader has to have a balance between staff well-being and what is best for the children. A leader has to ensure that they use the 1265 statute appropriately, but this does not mean that children lose out on experiences because of it.

Teaching is a difficult job and a time consuming one. Leaders have worked tirelessly over the last few years to support more proactive and time-efficient marking policies and assessment frameworks. Well-being of staff must be at the forefront of a leader's mind, but we must always remember that the school is for the children. They have one chance at education, and we must do everything in our power to make this a successful and rewarding time that opens doors for their future. A leader has to ensure that the balance is right, and their ethos and culture will determine that. Any environment where the staff needs far outweigh the needs of the children can be counterproductive.

As a leader I am passionate about staff well-being and making sure that staff feel valued and have a positive work-life balance. Staff need to feel safe, happy and rewarded in their roles. Developing a culture for staff well-being should be a key component of a leader's work, and a leader should do this with the staff not to them. Can you create a working group to discuss how staff feel and what the areas they are concerned about or need more support with?

Think about how you can develop a positive working ethos for staff. How can you celebrate excellence, hard work and say thank you for all the staff do?

Well-being isn't about yoga and meditation. It is about listening to staff, alleviating anxieties and showing them how valued and appreciated they are. Some may prefer yoga, but others will be happy with a simple 'thank you' or an adaptation of a policy to decrease workload. I have seen and been part of some great well-being initiatives such as:

- Staff Oscars
- Senior leadership team (SLT) breakfast
- Fantastic Friday awards for staff

One thing I know is that time is crucial for colleagues. Think how you can save it, not waste it, in your culture.

Core values

All the work you do as a leader of inclusion has to have the children at heart, and you must build your culture around this. As we move through the book you will see that the strategy involved in becoming a successful leader of inclusion has to be about building an ethos and a culture that is all about children.

The culture of a school is generally underpinned by core values.

> What are the core values that drive you?
> Have they ever changed?
> Will they ever change?

These are my core values:

- Integrity

- Honesty

- Fun

- Love

- Respect

- Determination

My core values embody everything that I do. I have to ensure that each day there is fun and enjoyment in my work, and that whatever I do as a leader there is fun and enjoyment in my setting. Alongside this, I have to work in an environment where people feel loved. This, in practice, means that they feel valued, listened to, trusted and that they can be themselves. Why wouldn't we want to feel like that on a daily basis?

I have these values as a school culture that is created by the experiences that children are part of. Experiences that we are part of drive the subsequent feelings, and those in turn impact on our behaviour.

It is why I always try and build ethos and values around love, fun and enjoyment. If children (and adults) are subjected to experiences that contain these values, it will make them feel much more positive, and they will behave and work in a different way.

This is why I feel we have an ever-growing issue with mental health in schools. Children are subjected to lots of testing and pressures, and become more anxious and nervous about failure. We have to balance the accountability and the exam pressures, but as a leader of inclusion make sure there are plenty of opportunities to celebrate, to have fun, to share love and satisfaction.

As you develop your ethos and communicate your key values in your setting, reflect on how you can ensure that they run through all aspects of the school. A broad and balanced curriculum is crucial to this; there will be lots of opportunities to embody your values within the curriculum.

Work with other leaders to ensure they are taught in different subjects and that direct reference is made to them so pupils can see the link. Work closely with the leader of PSHE and Religious Studies – how can you ensure your values are delivered through their curriculum offer?

Think about how you can communicate your values at every opportunity – are they visible in classrooms and corridors?

Are they mentioned in communication to parents and are they on your letterheads, your website and your social media platforms?

In order to fully establish your core values, they must be taught, experienced and celebrated through every aspect of school life.

Leading inclusion scenario one

You have been appointed as deputy head in a new school, and from your initial research and early work with the school it is clear that there are no common values across the school. The culture of the school needs re-launching as it has lost its way a little, and staff feel unsupported and children's behaviour can be challenging at times.

Reflect on what your key values are. How will you introduce these? Why are they so important to you and what do they mean in practice for your school?

Think strategically about how you will start a piece of work to create new values, a new ethos and embed a new culture. Who will you work with? How will you start the process and then embed it?

Operationally, how will you communicate these values and ensure that they are known and embedded throughout school?

2 Leadership – leading the line

Leading inclusion is a challenging but rewarding role. Each and every day you will be asked to make difficult decisions, and your leadership style and method will affect how you handle the situation. This chapter will focus on some of the different leadership styles that you could use in your role and it gives an insight into what each one is. The chapter will then look at some key leadership attributes that I think are crucial to be a successful leader of inclusion.

The second half of the chapter gives you an insight into strategic leadership and how to tie in your school development plan to your pastoral work. Operational leadership is a key part in this role, but you also need to delegate aspects to your team. The chapter gives an example of a structure that you may use to set up your pastoral team and how each tier of that structure supports you in your role. There are some thinking points for you to reflect on your leadership style. The scenario for the chapter is to draw up a strategic and operational plan post OFSTED regarding the provision for SEND pupils. As you move through the chapter think about what your strategy would be to address this and how might you achieve it operationally with your team and other staff.

What is leadership?

I love the challenges it brings, and I love the problem solving. As a leader I quickly found out that I spent most of my time dealing with adult problems rather than the children's. I was fortunate to be given extensive leadership training on my journey. I was also privileged to learn from excellent role models. What I try to ensure I do in my role now is to cascade my leadership knowledge and experience onto others and to ensure that we give adequate time and resources to train our current and aspiring leaders of the future.

To start this chapter, it is important we look at leadership.

- What is it? What traits do good and poor leaders have?
- What theory and research are there to guide us?

And most important of all:

- How can you lead a team effectively, both from a strategic and operational capacity, to support your ethos, values and culture?

Traits of leadership

What is effective leadership?

For me effective leadership is combining several key attributes well on a daily basis. A leader can be many things, but effective leadership is a constant demonstration of certain attributes.

Generally different types of leadership can be grouped according to these eight categories as defined by Charry, 2012.

Where would you put yourself in these theories?

As you develop your style and as you take more steps up the leadership ladder, people want to know who you are as a leader and how you lead others and adapt to different situations.

Type of leadership	Description
Great Man Theory	Great leaders are born, not made. They are heroic and mythic and destined to rise to leadership.
Trait Theory	People inherit certain qualities or traits that make them more suited to leadership. Particular traits or behaviour characteristics are shared by leaders.
Contingency Theory	Different environmental variables will dictate which type of leadership style is used. No single leadership style is appropriate in all situations.
Situational Theory	Leaders choose the best course of action based on the situation they are in. Also, certain leadership styles will be more prevalent in certain situations.
Behavioural Theory	Great leaders are made, not born. People learn to become leaders through training and observation.
Participative Theory	The preferred leadership style is the one that takes on board the input of others. Leaders encourage the participation and contributions from others.
Transactional/ Management Theory	Dictates that a leader's job is to create structures that make it clear what is expected of followers, both rewarding and consequential, based on meeting or not meeting expectations.
Relationship/ Transformational Theory	This is based around leaders creating a connection with their followers; they motivate and inspire others and focus on individuals' potential too. These leaders have high ethical and moral standards.

Thinking point one

Look at all the theories just listed and others, and reflect on where you are in each and start to understand yourself as a leader. This is crucial to becoming a successful leader: you have to know yourself and lead yourself first to become effective in leading others.

- Which leader do you think you are?
- Which leader would you like to become?

Jot down which boxes you fall into.

Key leadership attributes

To be an effective leader of inclusion these are the leadership attributes that I think you have to display daily. Anybody who is any good at anything has to have skills and attributes. A skill can develop over time. An attribute is innate; it embodies the leader and is something that makes that person who they are. What follows is what I think a leader of inclusion's key attributes should be.

These are **knowledge**, **drive**, being an **effective communicator** (this can be a skill; however, some people just possess the ability to do this well – forgive me for calling it an attribute!), **reflective**, **people focused** and **influential**.

Knowledge

This is purely in the behavioural theory camp. To be an effective leader of inclusion you have to have a detailed **knowledge** of all the key aspects of inclusion. An effective leader needs to understand behaviour: where it comes from, how you can change it, how you can manage it and how you can influence it. You need to have **knowledge** of SEN, the Code of Practice, the testing, the different codes of educational need and how you can go about getting support. You also need to have a good understanding of pedagogy and how SEN, behaviour and understanding can be supported by quality-first teaching. Alongside this you need to understand policy and law around attendance, exclusions and safeguarding. It is a complex and demanding job, and this is where a leader needs to build an effective team and delegate some of these operational responsibilities. You can't know everything, but you must have a **knowledge** of the basics and this has to be married to your ethos.

Finally, you need to have **knowledge** about yourself: what makes you tick, what your strengths and limitations are. Without a true **knowledge** of yourself you will find yourself becoming increasingly frustrated and ineffective. The more you understand yourself as a leader, the more you will manage the situations you find yourself in.

Drive

Drive is such an important attribute when leading inclusion. Firstly, how can you go about supporting children and helping them to overcome their barriers and difficulties if you have no **drive**? How can you lead a team of people to do the same without **drive**? An effective leader of inclusion has to be driven to make things better for themselves and for the children in their care. The role of a leader of inclusion is like a roller coaster. The emotional highs and lows are like nothing else, and you constantly have to pick yourself up and go again. Without **drive** this is not possible.

My good friend and ex-colleague created an anecdote for me that continues to resonate to this day and that I share frequently with our team.

> Leading is like being a snowman. Each day you get worn down (melt) a little bit more and no matter how much has been worn away you have to go home and rebuild that snowman so that you are ready and prepared for the next day.

Effective communicator

Communication is key.

> If you fail with communication, you fail with everything else.
>
> (Lukas Karwacki)

As a senior leader it is vital that we **communicate** with all stakeholders. Being an **effective communicator** is a key attribute to possess when leading in a pastoral role. As discussed earlier you need to over-communicate at times. Do everything within your power to do this.

Can you use:

- Weekly assemblies?
- Social media?
- House competitions?
- Value word weeks?
- Your planner?

Once children and staff get a daily diet of the same communication, it becomes the norm.

One of the most important actions to regularly participate in is **communicating** to the staff body about the children. There is nothing more frustrating for a teacher or associate professional than finding out about a new pupil starting that day, or even worse to be stood in front of them in your class that day. As a leader you need to think carefully how you want to **communicate** the information and to decide what information to give and what it is related to. A few topics to think about may be:

- New starters/in-year admissions
- Y6-Y7 transition
- Managed move children (see later chapter)
- SEND information/one-page profiles/Education, Health and Care Plan
- Behaviour plans
- Bereavement updates
- Safeguarding updates

The vehicle that you wish to deliver this information through is also really important. Too little information is equally as frustrating as information overload. A briefing, for example, can be the perfect vehicle to pass information on. You have the whole staff body. However, if you talk too long, are not succinct, or if it's at the end of a long day, then it could be a wasted opportunity. Think how you can share the information so that colleagues get what they need and understand what needs to be done with it and do it in a timely manner. Here are a few examples I have used or seen colleagues use:

- Weekly staff briefing – 30-second update on safeguarding concerns; a quick update on children to watch for and support
- SEND newsletter – weekly updates sent out by the SENDCO that share information about pupils on the register and strategies to support them
- Vulnerable Learner Network – a meeting held weekly to discuss pupils who are vulnerable; minutes and actions of this meeting are shared with staff
- Interventions meeting – a weekly meeting where all staff can refer to pupils that are causing them concern or where they can find out about their home life or situation
- New starter blog – a weekly short piece about new starters, their needs, their current attainment levels and any other information. This blog also contains information on any pupils who have left the school
- Half termly pastoral review – a detailed update of attendance, behaviour and achievements. This is also the chance to highlight the details of pupils who are currently on or about to be on managed moves, and the dates of when they start/finish or are reviewed

Whatever means you decide to use, always remember to speak to your colleagues and find out how they would prefer to receive the information and what works best for your setting.

An important aside to **communication** is that we need to realise that there are several forms. One of these key forms you will need as a senior leader, particularly in a pastoral setting, is to listen! Staff will come with issues and concerns, will need reassurance and will need guidance. Make the time for them; listen and listen well. A good leader has their ear to the ground and needs to instil a sense of trust with their staff. You need to be approachable and welcoming.

Reflective

To be an effective leader we have identified you need knowledge, experience and drive. You also need to have a level of authenticity or gravitas. This leads me to a quote I use a lot in leadership sessions. It is about being self-aware and understanding who you are as a leader.

> Authenticity requires self-awareness. Self-awareness requires reflection.
> (Dan Rockwell – Leadership Freak blog)

Without true and purposeful **reflection**, how will a leader ever learn from mistakes, or learn more about themselves and the situations they face?

Reflecting is a skill and needs practice, but I would urge you to reflect on all you do. Build in a slot each week in your diary and choose an hour where you can sit quietly and reflect on the week and how you can learn from all the events that have occurred.

One of the most powerful things I have done was part of a leadership day we did as a SLT. The idea was for us to look at our successes, strengths and areas to develop. This little task we did resonated with me and I have used it ever since. It's quite difficult for people to do and you need to have established some trust and positive relationships with your team.

Everyone has five minutes to write down two or three things that are real strengths of each team member and why they are strengths. You also need to include one thing for them to work on. You then set up the room like a 'speed-dating' event and you get up to one minute to talk about the three strengths and the area to work on and then swap. You then move around and speak to each other person in turn. I found this very rewarding and it allowed me to reflect a lot on what I was good at and what I may need to work on.

Never stop **reflecting**, never stop learning about yourself and never think you have learnt everything.

People focused

One of the most important attributes that I focus on is being **people focused** or centred. The staff body are the collective cog that make school a safe and meaningful place for our children. If we can ensure our staff are supported and happy in their work, then our children will be the same.

Being **people focused** is a key attribute and one that not every leader, new or experienced, may necessarily focus on.

As a leader of inclusion, you have to get this right. Staff who work within inclusion will have emotionally charged days. There will be the elation of success and downright depression of lows. It is our job as a leader to look out for our colleagues and make sure we support them, advise them and give them a break where needed. In your teams you will have associate professionals whose job range could be:

- Administrative support
- Non-teaching head of year
- Attendance lead
- Teaching assistant
- Assistant SENDCO
- Safeguarding lead
- Behaviour worker
- Mental health worker

You will then also have teaching colleagues whose roles, alongside teaching a quite substantial timetable, could be:

- SENDCO
- Assistant SENDCO
- Head of year
- Attainment leader
- Pupil Premium Champion

All of these colleagues will feel the push and pull factors of their day-to-day job and they will all also be part of smaller teams within your setting. All of these colleagues will have different 'drivers' for their work and all will need supporting, pushing and developing in different ways. By being **people focused** you will naturally learn to speak to them every day. You need to get to know them all as individuals. Think about the following questions:

- What makes them tick?
- What frustrates them?
- How do they lead?
- How do they communicate?
- What are their strengths?
- What are their areas to develop?
- How do they like to be led by others?

It is your job to find out these things and lead these people on a daily basis. You will not get it right all the time; remember to reflect. Most importantly, though, make time for them. We are all busy, but they need your time, your experience and your ear.

I like to have a daily meeting over coffee. Get your team together, discuss the day and what they are all facing, offer your support and also use the time to chat about their lives and to have fun. Many of these meetings have included playing a practical joke on another colleague – teams need to bond and trust one other, and laughter is a great way to do this.

Empathetic leadership

One thing that is at the forefront of all I do when dealing with people is to be kind to them. It is one of my key values and something that I try and do each and every day. I hear stories where people are mistreated by leaders and I feel nothing but sympathy for those colleagues. If someone makes a mistake, we have to identify it, reflect and learn from it, and it is our job as leaders to facilitate that. Show empathy in all you do.

People love praise, it makes people feel valued and that resonates within. We try and do this with our children on a daily basis but, remember, as a **people-focused** person you need to focus on your team too: praise and reward them when it is required. One key message I took from an ex-head teacher of mine is that the written word is such a powerful way to say thank you. Every half term I write a thank you card to each member of my team to tell them how much I appreciate their work and what I think of them. Try it.

I also give them small tokens of my gratitude:

- A scratch card
- A lucky dip
- A bottle of wine
- An Easter egg
- A Christmas or holiday present

It is money and time well spent. As a leader you are nothing without the people you lead; look out for them, support them and make sure you challenge them. If you can take one thing from this book that has helped shape me as a leader and given me success, it has been about being **people focused**.

People-focused well-being strategies

Promoting well-being and ensuring staff have positive mental health is an area you must focus on. Think about how you can be creative and use ideas that will make people feel valued and rewarded.

Following are a few ideas/events/strategies that I have used or seen other colleagues create.

- Fantastic Friday – pupils nominate adults weekly by writing a message on a card. One is pulled out and the staff member wins a prize. All messages are passed back to staff. This can go all over social media!
- SLT breakfast – this is something I have done in both my current and previous school. Every half term on the last or penultimate day, SLT cook breakfast for the staff body.
- House events – create a purposeful house system and have staff competitions and prizes, including booby prizes. Have these often and make them fun and enjoyable.
- Staff-specific requests – in previous schools I have asked staff what they would like to be provided with that would help. We have done the following:
  - Car valet
  - Ironing
  - Manicures
- Well-being group – create a working group who can speak to staff and generate ideas for events.
- Staff association – create an association where everyone pays an annual subscription and from that the staff body buys gifts for big events. You can fund things like staff BBQs or little giveaways each half term.
- Be creative with INSET days – have some twilights and then give extra days off on scheduled INSET days at Christmas time, February half term and so on.
- Nativity plays – work together as a staff body so that all staff can go and watch their child in a play – cover each other on these occasions.
- Staff events – make sure you do whole staff events like World Book Day, Sports Day, bake-offs and so on. It brings everyone together.

Thinking point two

Jot down the answers to these questions:
- What do you do for your team?
- What does your leader do for you?
- What does the school do for you all?

Influential

So, what does it mean to be **influential** or to have **influence** over others?

The dictionary defines influence as:

the capacity to have an effect on the character, development or behaviour of someone or something.

Does every leader need this attribute?
Absolutely.

If you are going to shape your team, bring about change and take people with you on that journey, then you must be influential. This attribute is a necessity for a leader of inclusion. Without influencing the people you work with, how can you create your vision? How can these people become your team if you have no influence over them? Without **influence** in a school, how can you positively affect the lives of children?

When I think about **influence** it brings me back full circle to what we discussed in Chapter 1: values and ethos. If you are driven by key values and an ethos that people can 'feel', then they will buy into these and into you as a leader, thus starting your **influence**.

One way to build your **influence** is to do what the title of this chapter states: lead the line. Put simply this is 'sweating the small things' and 'walking the talk' – you must be prepared to do what you ask others to do.

You also have to be a role model to those around you. You have to:

- Inspire

- Motivate

- Challenge

- Develop others

- Give success

Consistent application of these attributes will see your **influence** grow. To be truly influenced by you as a leader these beliefs need to align to the staff's. Some people may not be influenced by you and they may not buy into what you are striving for. These people may leave the team you are building, as they don't see themselves fitting with what you are creating. They are influenced by other ideas and other people. This is fine.

A leader of inclusion needs a team who believes in what they do. Use your **influence** to get the right people in the right seats on your journey to success. Make sure you tell them where you are heading. People need to see the end goal; they need success. It breeds confidence and it develops habit. The big picture needs to be shared.

Effort and courage are not enough without purpose and direction.
(John F. Kennedy)

The next part of this chapter focuses on the way you can get the big picture across and the two methods of leadership that as a leader of inclusion you have to switch between on a daily basis.

Strategic leadership

Strategic leadership is one of the most important skills needed as a senior leader of inclusion. It is the vehicle to share your big picture and see how your team's work contributes to whole-school improvement. It is the way to align their work and to be able to build a quality assurance process that verifies what you are doing well. Strategic leadership allows you to focus on key areas to improve and ensures that everyone is on the same page and not working in isolation. The ability to plan your work so that it dovetails and supports the whole school is crucial. There are several key drivers that will influence your strategy in leading inclusion. These are:

- The school improvement plan
- OFSTED
- Trust goals/improvement plan
- Governance

The key influencer for me is an effective school improvement plan.

School improvement plans (SIPs)

Every school that you work in will have one of these. The idea and purpose of a SIP is to identify what key areas you are going to focus on over the coming academic year and what you will embed or improve. These plans tend to refer to and have headings that are associated with the current OFSTED framework. This gives you a platform to demonstrate how you are meeting the requirements for each heading and it allows you to align the work of the full staff body. You will be given certain areas to lead and improve, and it is crucial that you share these and delegate aspects of them to your team – the bigger picture!

SIPs will vary in every school. Some will be 30-page documents, some will be one page. A lot will depend on the school's position regarding OFSTED and its performance. The length of the document will also depend on the head teacher's style of leadership. So long as there are clear aims, objectives and projected improvements, the size doesn't matter. If it is effective in bringing about positive change, then keep it. However, it must have a level of clarity and a clear purpose that everyone can read and understand.

Every leader in the school should see it and know what it is aiming to do and where their role fits within it. They should produce a development plan for the area they lead, and they can then tie in the work of their colleagues. They will also use this information to support their own appraisal and performance management. This is the way strategic leadership drives the work of an entire staff body and results in everyone working towards the same goals – strategic teamwork at its best.

One-page improvement plans

Having worked with long detailed plans and one-page ones too, I must say I prefer a one-page one. In one of my previous schools, we worked over three days with OFSTED inspectors to see how we could design a one-page plan. It was one of the best pieces of training I have had, and I now use this as much as I can. We altered the format a little to suit us and as a team we designed a new format. An example of a one-page plan is shown in Figure 2.1.

This is my pastoral development plan. Across the top are the key performance indicators used to measure progress and aligned to the OFSTED framework. Under each heading are further goals giving clarity about what needs to be achieved. Then further below, each leader of each year group has created two targets to achieve over the academic year for each category. This ensures all my teams are working towards the same goals and I can focus our work and quality assure it.

Each member of staff is a 'strategic enabler' and is responsible for two or three targets. Every half term I send out the form shown in Figure 2.2 and they have to present detail about the progress made towards the target. They can summarise their progress, but I also need to see the evidence of the work undertaken that is either stapled to the sheet or sent electronically. As the staff are using these targets for their appraisal it helps them to keep an evidence trail too. At our review meetings we can then write in what further actions need to take place to improve whatever the target is. Figure 2.2 is a reward example.

This method of working will allow you to keep a strategic plan and have evidence that shows the impact of your work. I then use this information when feeding back to SLT, the trust and our governors. It is also a great base to start any discussions with OFSTED inspectors.

Operational leadership

As a senior leader for inclusion you will also complete a lot of operational leadership work. This work is equally as important as the strategic side, especially when you are new to the role or the school. This is where you 'lead the line' and ensure you support all your colleagues and get your hands dirty, so to speak.

A word of caution though: if you are not careful you can be pulled into every aspect of the operational day and you simply can't do this. Make sure that you build clear tiers of responsibility within your teams and ensure that when children or parents have issues that you follow these tiers, or you will find yourself dealing with every situation and attending every meeting. If they really need you for support in a parental meeting or similar, they will tell you, but you must not let your team members pass everything to you. They need to understand that they have a responsibility within the team structure to tackle issues and to hold difficult

Pastoral DeliveryPlan – Creating and Owning Your Culture

Leading in Academy Education	Driving a Culture of Excellence	Driving Social Equity and Responsibility	Driving Expertise & Innovation
KPI 1: Attendance/Punctuality	**KPI 2: Behaviour and Attitudes**	**KPI 3: Personal Development**	**KPI 4: Leadership and Management**
Goal 2: Attendance has improved quickly and is broadly in line with national. The new strategy delivers impact and thorough support where needed. Persistent absenteeism has declined and is broadly in line with national.	*Students and staff behave consistently well, with high levels of respect for others with no tolerance of bullying, harassment or violence. Attitudes are positive and students play an active part in supporting others and their Academy community.*	*Students are confident, self-assured learners. Their excellent attitudes to learning have a strong, positive impact on their progress. They are proud of their achievements and of their school.*	*Leaders have created a culture that enables students to excel. They are committed unwaveringly to setting high expectations for the conduct of students. Relationships between staff and students are exemplary and their leadership dictates this.*
Students recognise the importance of attendance and regularly attend school. The arrive on time to school and lessons 'a strong focus on attendance and punctuality l'Year and effective behaviour and punctuality so that disruption is minimised' **Year group goals** 1.1 To achieve 94% attendance for the year group by the end of the year 1.2 To reduce the number of lates to lesson in particular to P4c 1.3 Attendance in Y8 to be at least 92.5% by the end of the year 1.4 Reduce lates for Y8 pupils in a morning 1.5 To achieve a minimum of 92% attendance for Y9 at the end of the academic year 1.6Reduce Tutor time and lesson truancy on a half termly by half termly basis 1.7Reduce Internal truancy at tutor time 1.8Increase attendance to 93% by the end of the academic year. Supporting document provided 1.9 Y11 attendance to be 93%" by the end of the year 1.10 To ensure internal truancy of Y11 is eradicated from Christmas	*Students are equipped with behaviours and attitudes ready for the next stage of their lives.* Goal 1: The leadership of behavior and attitudes is strong. Strong and consistent policies are followed fairly and demonstrate impact. Classroom removals show a declining trend Goal 3: Internal figures indicate that there is a declining picture for FTE over time. 5% in term two, 10% by term three. Repeat offenders are supported with clear graduated responses to support a rapid improvement in behaviour. Disadvantaged FTE gap is reduced by 15% Goal 4: Safeguarding is effective. Pupils report they feel safe and there a numerous interventions, both clinical and therapeutic that support mental health. Effective strategies are in place for pupils to be and feel safe in school, in the community and on-line. **Year group goals** 2.1 To improve the behaviour and attitude of key pupils through rewards, strategies & consequences; monitored through the number of on-calls and FTEs 2.2 To reduce the number of 'on-call' pastoral issues and peer conflicts 2.3 Reports and competitions between students for repeat FTE to look to reduce them 2.4 Reduce removals from HT 1 - HTG in Y8 2.5 Reduce FTEs in Year Year 9 by 10% per term 2.6 Use on call data to identify hotspots and use strategies and IRIS to reduce on calls 2.7 Named cohort with aim to reduce 'on calls' and increase successes 2.8 To reduce the number of FTE's using a graduated response. 2.9 FTEs in Y11 decrease by 10% in term 2 and 20% in term 3 2.10 Y11 pupils are punctual to lessons and prepared for school evidenced through QA	*The school provides a wide range of opportunities to nurture, develop and stretch pupils' talents and interests. The school provides high-quality pastoral support.* Goal 1: Pupil voice, pupil behaviour and attitudinal data indicates how pupils feel about the school. The House and reward system systematically celebrates successes and promotes a community feel Goal 2: Pupils develop and indicate resilience to problems and are able to involve themselves in projects and extra-curricular activities that develop their character **Year group goals** 3.1 Provide further roles and responsibilities for Y7 form reps to organise an event and promote a sense of identity and community as a tutor group and year group 3.2 Promote the house system and competition through inter form or inter house competitions, using rewards 3.3 Celebrate achievements for the consistently good students in a variety of ways 3.4 Raise achievement points and reduce behaviour points for all pupils in lessons 3.5 Raise the amount of achievement points and lower the behaviour points in Y9 term on term 3.6 Develop rewards for achievement points out of lesson for highest achievers to promote positive attitudes 3.7 Secure 16 student counsellors (2 from each form) voted for by each form group 3.8Set up 'student voice' - meeting 12/12/19 3.9 Celebrate success and reward excellence through a variety of methods 3.10 Develop student voice for the year group through work with the prefects	*Leaders create an atmosphere for students to excel. They are numerous opportunities to lead, succeed and try new experiences* 'leadership opportunities are created at all levels. Pupils contribute to their form time, year group and House systems Leaders plan to encourage and develop leaders' 'Leaders systematically quality assure their work and ensure all pupils are given the best experiences in their care' **Year team goals** 4.1Challenge HAPs/MAPs to provide new learning experiences and opportunities to lead and achieve success 4.2QA delivery of character education, attendance tracking, standards and expectations, behavior monitoring and rewards through tutor time and tutor meetings. 4.3 Head boy and Head Girl - application and interviews for Y8 4.4 Plan and deliver LGBTQ+ for year 8 and then whole school - through assemblies 4.5 Pupils to contribute to tutor time, leading sessions, pupil voice. 4.6 Plan and develop a strategy to create form representatives that meet regularly to voice any pupil concerns or projects 4.7 Use the House captains effectively in tutor time and year assemblies 4.8Push equality by re advertising for a larger team, recruiting males and rebranding as yr10 prefects 4.9 CEIAC for post 16 - develop opportunities and information through tutor time, U explore, pupil voice, interviews, 4.10 Develop an active and purposeful prefect and leadership group

Key Themes, KPIs and Goals

To have oversight of and be responsible for:

- Standards in your year group
- Behaviour in your group
- Attendance in your year group
- Development and leadership in your year group

Strategic Enablers

NCR	SCO
JSM	JHA
NKI	RMO
RWO	
GMU	
AGI	
MRO	

Figure 2.1 Example of a one-page Pastoral Improvement Plan

KPI Pastoral Tracker

	KPI	Strategic Enablers	Feb half term	May half term	Summer term
1.1	To achieve 94% attendance for the year group by the end of the year	NCR			
1.2	2 To reduce the number of lates to lesson in particular to P4c	NCR/JSM			
1.3	Attendance in Y8 to be at least 92.5% by the end of the year	NKI/RWO			
1.4	Reduce lates for Y8 pupils in a morning	NKI/RWO			
1.5	To achieve a minimum of 92% attendance for Y9 at the end of the academic year	GMU			
1.6	Reduce Tutor time and lesson truancy on a half termly by half termly basis	AGI			
1.7	Reduce internal truancy at tutor time	MRO/SCO			
1.8	Increase attendance to 93% by the end of the academic year. Supporting document	MRO			
1.9	Y11 attendance to be 93%* by the end of the year	RMO			
1.10	To ensure internal truancy of Y11 is eradicated from Christmas	RMO			
2.1	1 To improve the behaviour and attitude of key pupils through rewards, strategies & consequences; monitored through the number of on-calls and FTEs	NCR/JSM			
2.2	To reduce the number of 'on-call' pastoral issues and peer conflicts	NCR/JSM			
2.3	Reports and competitions between students for repeat FTE to look to reduce them	NKI/RWO			
2.4	Reduce removals from HT 1 – HT6 in Y8	NKI/RWO			
2.5	Reduce FTEs in Year 9 by 10% per term	AGI			
2.6	Use on call data to identify hotspots and use strategies and IRIS to reduce on calls	AGI/GMU			
2.7	Named cohort with aim to reduce 'on calls' and increase successes	SCO/MRO			
2.8	To reduce the number of FTE's using a graduated response.	SCO/MRO			
2.9	FTEs in Y11 decrease by 10% in term 2 and 20% in term 3	JHA/SPR			
2.10	Y11 pupils are punctual to lessons and prepared for school evidenced through QA	JHA/SPR			
3.1	Provide further roles and responsibilities for Y7 form reps to organise an event and promote a sense of identity and community as a tutor group and year group	NCR			
3.2	Promote the house system and competition through inter form or inter house competitions, using rewards (JSM).	JSM			
3.3	Celebrate achievements for the consistently good students in a variety of ways	NKI/RWO			
3.4	Raise achievement points and reduce behaviour points for all pupils in lessons	NKI/RWO			
3.5	Raise the amount of achievement points and lower the behaviour points in Y9 term on term	AGI/GMU			
3.6	Develop rewards for achievement points out of lesson for highest achievers to promote positive attitudes	AGI/GMU			
3.7	Secure 16 student counsellors (2 from each form) voted for by each form group	MRO			
3.8	Set up 'student voice' – meeting 12/12/19	MRO/SCO			
3.9	Celebrate success and reward excellence through a variety of methods	RMO			

Figure 2.1a (Continued)

24 Leadership – leading the line

3.10	Develop student voice for the year group through work with the prefects	JHA					
4.1	Challenge HAPs/MAPs to provide new learning experiences and opportunities to lead and achieve success (NCR).	NCR					
4.2	QA delivery of character education, attendance tracking, standards and expectations, behavior monitoring and rewards through tutor time and tutor meetings	NCR/JSM					
4.3	Head boy and Head Girl - application and interviews for Y8	NKI/RWO					
4.4	Plan and deliver LGBTQ+ for year 8 and then whole school – through assemblies	NKI/RWO					
4.5	Pupils to contribute to tutor time, leading sessions, pupil voice.	GMU					No evidence
4.6	Plan and develop a strategy to create form representatives that meet regularly to voice any pupil concerns or projects	GMU					No evidence
4.7	Use the House captains effectively in tutor time and year assemblies	SCO					
4.8	Push equality by re advertising for a larger team, recruiting males and rebranding as yr10 prefects	MRO					No evidence
4.9	CEIAG for post 16 - develop opportunities and information through tutor time, U explore, pupil voice, interviews.	RMO					
4.10	Develop an active and purposeful prefect and leadership group	RMO/JHA					No evidence

Figure 2.1b (Continued)

Delivery Plan Feedback 2019-20

Strategic Enabler/s: Mark Allen   **½ term:**   1

Delivery Plan KPI   Rewards systems are developed through the House and through Pastoral strategies (Hot choc Friday, 100% awards)

R/A/G

Evidence
Please cite specific actions that have taken place, impact of actions (with reference to data improvements where possible) and further actions that are to be taken.

Rewards system in place
Staff can log House points of varying degrees.
Positive on-call used by staff
26,452 positive points logged to date by staff.

House system co-ordinator job in place. Weekly slides sent to indicate points scorers and House leaders. Weekly House competitions organised and participation of them encouraged.
House badges and House shop operating and monitored by House lead

Individual rewards given by different year leads and departments - these include queue jump passes, form tutor breakfast, extra-curricular trips, ice-cream van, attendance awards

Whole year groups awards given at half term in October
End of Year awards evenings planned, end of year Sports Presentation Evening planned.
Half termly and termly attendance vouchers given

Weekly hot choc Friday awards with pupils - 85 different pupils nominated. All receive postcards and 30 House points.

<u>Actions required to futher improve</u>
Promote and push house week events more
Develop more lesson based rewards - meet with Department heads to create a school offer of rewards
Invite Class charts to present to SLT and investigate its use to support rewards next year
Obtain pupil voice from each year group about rewards for next year
Interview House captains and create pupil survey for rewards

Figure 2.2 Strategic enabler evidence form for rewards

conversations and meetings too. When I started my new roles, I went to the first meeting or two with every member of staff and chaired them; that way I could model what I wanted these meetings to be like and it allowed my colleagues to gain experience by watching and listening.

Inclusion staffing structure

The structure of your inclusion/pastoral teams will dictate how many tiers you have, and it is important as a senior leader that you regularly review your team structure with the head teacher and ensure you have enough people in the right positions.

In a school, you have to invest in your inclusion team. It doesn't matter how fabulous your teachers are and how good teaching and learning is; if you haven't got the required wrap-around support for these pupils, then they will not be able to regulate or learn in lessons. What follows is a typical structure that I have used in settings. It is expensive, but it needs to be. This is where you are creative, and you ensure that some of the funding comes from all the pots you have available. Make sure you liaise with your Pupil Premium Champion and your SENDCO; they will have funding streams that you can use.

Tier 1

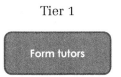

The role of the form tutor is crucial and often overlooked quite a lot in settings today. Your heads of year should be leading their form tutors to be the most important and first port of call for their children, empowering them to take actions and be responsible for their children. They should also be involved in phone calls home for positive and negative reasons, and they meet parents too. Tier 1 strategies to help are things like form tutor reports and reward charts. Your tutors should be reviewing inclusion data on a weekly basis and helping to identify issues and put in Wave One support of a graduated response.

Tier 2

This second tier is the engine room. These are the colleagues who on a daily basis, as part of their roles, will be picking up issues and dealing with them. They will be liaising with parents, with other teaching staff and outside agencies. Make sure you are available to discuss things with them and support where necessary. Depending on the experience of these colleagues, you will decide on how much you can delegate and how much support you can offer. Part of my leadership style is to empower my team, make sure I give them the experiences they need, challenge them and push them to do the difficult jobs. They will appreciate it.

An assistant SENDCO is a key role in your structure. They are the ones who link pastoral and SEND together. You need to regularly liaise with the SENDCO. This colleague is your conduit to that. They can help to initiate support for behaviour and support for learning and can start to support your work with outside agencies such as:

- Educational psychologists
- Speech and language therapists
- Mental health workers
- Counsellors

A weekly meeting with this colleague and/or the SENDCO is crucial. This tier of people is critical to developing an appropriate and child-centred approach.

When I started leading inclusion I had to do a lot of training and continuous professional development (CPD) on safeguarding and child protection. I was fortunate that I could also learn from one of the best colleagues I have worked with. A safeguarding lead to pick up and deal with daily concerns is a crucial role in Tier 2.

Tier 3

SENDCO | Assistant Head teachers | Inclusion Lead

This final tier is the one that will work more closely on the strategy with you, but they are also crucial to the operational side of things. An inclusion lead is a key cog in a big team. They are the one who line manages, supports and works closely with all your heads of year. They have oversight of your day-to-day running, including data. This is generally an associate professional as they need to have the time to support, organise and lead meetings while liaising with you. These roles are really important as they also give associate staff the opportunity to develop and progress professionally.

In this role you will work with and possibly line manage other senior leaders. These relationships are critical – they need to be on the same page as you, they need to see the bigger picture and they need to drive a lot of your work. They will also have a relatively high teaching load so it is your job to support them where you can, but equally you have to empower them to lead and develop their skills. You must challenge them and push them hard to pick up and lead key work, and also to be the final tier between any burning issues and you. This is your closest team; you need to build and develop trust and know how each one of them works. This tier is where your line management is so important. Meet them every week, check how they are, check their work against the improvement plan and make sure they are working on the big picture. These colleagues should then be line managing the tier below and disseminating the same messages each week.

Make sure you build a close working relationship with your SENDCO. They hold the keys to extra support for children in lessons and around school. They have the evidenced-based knowledge to assist you. If you have a child that is displaying challenging behaviour, patterns of removals from lessons or pupils not making enough progress in lessons, speak to your SENDCO. They can help with assessing any learning barriers that may be present, and administer tests and allocate extra resource and support. You need to always have in your thought process why children are behaving the way they are: what are they trying to communicate? I have worked with some excellent SENDCOs. They are experts in their field and will help you to no end with your inclusive strategy. If you are to build an ethos that is child-centred and inclusive, then this is the colleague who needs to have the same mentality, ethos and values as you.

Tier 4

Once all of your team and other tiers have done all they can, have initiated graduated responses and have used external agencies, they may come to you. You should then be involved to support colleagues who may have issues with parents or external partners. If a parent is unhappy with all the previous tiers, it should then be up to you as the senior leader to sort out their concerns. Don't forget all these tiers, and finally you, are the buffers for the head teacher.

A good senior leader of inclusion will protect the head teacher from being involved in the majority of cases. You are the final cog to sort out any issues before it lands at the head teacher's door. You need to pull on all the advice, support and interventions used from all the tiers below before looking at the next steps. You must back your team and reinforce what they have said, unless you feel there have been a few errors or parts missed. This is where honesty and humility come in – it is okay to say we got things wrong and we need to try something else. But never, ever undermine or belittle a colleague's work in front of anyone.

Leading inclusion scenario two

Your school has just had its latest OFSTED inspection and an area to improve is to ensure SEND children have enough support in lessons. OFSTED identified a lack of provision and a lack of understanding of the difficulties they face. Your head teacher has asked you to come up with a strategy to improve the experiences and learning SEND pupils get at your school.

Outline what the strategy may look like.

Who will you work with? Think of your school's senior and middle leadership structure. Think about your pastoral team and how they can support this too.

What plans would need to be drawn up?
How will you measure the impact of your work?
Who will be operationally and strategically supportive to you?

Further reading

There are lots of books and research that focus on leadership. Following are some I highly recommend:

Buck, A. (2016). *Leadership Matters: How Leaders at All Levels Can Create Great Schools.* Jon Catt Educational Limited.

Rees, T. (2018). *Wholesome Leadership: The Heart, Head, Hands and Health of School Leaders.* Jon Catt Educational Limited.

Tierney, S. (2016). *Liminal Leadership: Building Bridges Across the Chaos . . . Because We Are Standing on the Edge.* Jon Catt Educational Limited.

Chapter 2 references and research

Charry, K. (2012). *Leadership Theories – 8 Major Leadership Theories.* http://psychology.about.com/od/leadership/p/leadtheories.htm. Cited in: Amanchukwu, R., Stanley, G., and Ololube, P. (2015). *A Review of Leadership Theories, Principles and Styles and Their Relevance to Educational Management.* www.researchgate.net/publication/283081945_A_Review_of_Leadership_Theories_Principles_and_Styles_and_Their_Relevance_to_Educational_Management

Rockwell, D. (2015). *Leadership Freak Blog.* https://leadershipfreak.blog/2015/10/02/powerful-tools-for-reflection-and-connection/

3 SEND and supporting your SENDCO

This chapter will focus on what SEND is, what your role as a leader of inclusion is with regard to SEND, and what strategic and operational processes you may find yourself part of or leading. You need to know who your SEND cohorts are, and as a key group in terms of accountability measures, your head teacher, governors and trust will want to know how they are being supported and how they are performing. This chapter will also look briefly at the Code of Practice that the government introduced in 2014 which radically changed the approach to SEND in schools. The main focus will be on how you understand and contribute to the work in SEND and, more importantly, how you can successfully lead, challenge and support your SENDCO.

The scenario at the end focuses on deficit hours and not enough provision for a group of SEND pupils and the impact that this has on school outcomes. As you work through the chapter think how your leadership can impact on SEND provision, the approach the school has and how you can influence the outcomes of SEND pupils in school. Think about how you approach teaching and learning, specific interventions and how you spend SEND funding to support children.

I am not going to focus on SEND as an entity but will dedicate time in this chapter to guide you on how to lead, assist and contribute to the work in SEND. The overlap between pastoral and SEND needs to be acknowledged and can be paramount in providing support for the holistic needs of the pupil.

Code of Practice 2014

The SEN Code of Practice is a piece of statutory guidance from the UK government for organisations that work with children who may have special education needs and disabilities. The guidance sets out duties, policies and procedures that establishments need to follow relating to the Children and Families Act 2014. Schools are obviously key organisations within this guidance.

The key changes that were made were the following:

- The Code of Practice covers the 0-25 age range

- It includes guidance that is related to children that have disabilities as well as those with SEN

- It empowers parents and children to be key stakeholders in the decision-making processes that influence their future choices

- It is clear that there should be a strong focus on high aspirations and outcomes for children

- It highlights how education, social care and health should work in collaboration

- It states that establishments should produce a 'local offer' that indicates what their establishment can offer for young people and how they can be supported.

- It indicates that schools should take a *graduated response* to identifying and supporting pupils with SEND

- It highlights and clarifies the process for children with more complex needs and how the evidence in graduated responses will help contribute to children progressing or ultimately being awarded an Education, Health and Care Plan (EHCP), which replaced the old statement of special educational need

- It develops a cohesive practice between health and educators which promotes clarity in a multi-agency approach to supporting vulnerable pupils

- It supports in the key transitional periods for pupils with additional needs

The four categories that children can be classified as having a special educational need changed and became:

- Communication and interaction

- Cognition and learning

- Social, emotional and mental health

- Sensory and/or physical needs

The Code of Practice was very clear that there should be a higher expectation placed on educational provisions for children with SEND needs, ensuring that no excuses were being made for a lack of progress or any lowering of expectations. School leaders should ensure they have made best endeavours to support pupils achieving in line with their peers.

The Code stipulates that:

Academies are required to use their best endeavours to ensure that the necessary provision is made for *any individual* who has SEN.

This should resonate with your **ethos and values** as a leader, as we discussed in Chapter 1. If you are going to successfully lead inclusion, then children should

Cognition and learning	Communication and interaction
Specific Learning Difficulties (SpLD)	Speech, language and communication needs
– Dyslexia	Asperger's syndrome and autism
– Dyscalculia	
– Dyspraxia	
– Moderate Learning Difficulty	
Social, emotional and mental health difficulties	**Sensory/or physical**
Social and emotional difficulties which may include becoming withdrawn or isolated, as well as displaying behaviour; ADD, ADHD or attachment disorder	– Vision impairment
	– Hearing impairment
	– Multi-sensory impairment
	– A disability which prevents or hinders them from making the facilities generally provided

be at the heart of everything you do. Children with SEND needs should be at the forefront of your thoughts, your strategic leadership and your long-term plan and the structure of your teams should reflect this. You need to ensure you work closely with your teaching and learning colleagues too as there is clear indication in the Code of Practice about the responsibility and accountability of teachers who teach children with SEND. This is crucial and has to be driven on all angles from the senior leadership team.

Too often, in previous years, children with SEND needs were taken out of classes, left to be supported by teaching assistants and other less qualified staff as we didn't invest enough time, thought and support into helping them. We also failed to support their teachers to understand what their difficulties were and how teachers could work with teaching assistants to support these needs. The teaching profession has had the professional training in pedagogical processes to support learning, therefore we should be driving the teaching of these children and supporting their learning. Focus needs to be placed on ensuring that quality-first teaching is provided, resulting in the progress of all learners.

Thinking point one

In the Code of Practice 2014, every teacher is responsible and accountable for all pupils in their class wherever or with whoever the pupils are working. Reflect on your current school or previous places of work.

- How are/were SEN children supported in class?
- Are/were they 'velcro'd' to a TA?
- Did/do they work with you?
- How regularly did/do you liaise with and join up with your TAs?

■ Did/does your TA take groups of pupils out of your class? Why?

■ Would it not be better for the teacher, with the qualifications, pedagogical knowledge and experience, to take a group who needs more support and the TA take the rest of the class?

■ Why doesn't this happen more?

■ What are your thoughts about this?

Jot down your thoughts about these questions.

Learning without Limits

So, what can we promote in our classrooms? How, as a leader of inclusion, can you support your colleagues? The key is **communication**, one of our key leadership attributes. We must communicate our professional expectations of staff and what we require them to do. We must have a clear strategy on how we will support the staff to ensure that children with SEND can access the learning and make progress academically and socially.

This is what a good strategic model for what teaching SEND and supporting children should look like. This is taken from the Code of Practice; it's not anything revolutionary and, remember, we need to maintain clarity and keep things concise. A method to communicate effectively is using visual diagrams.

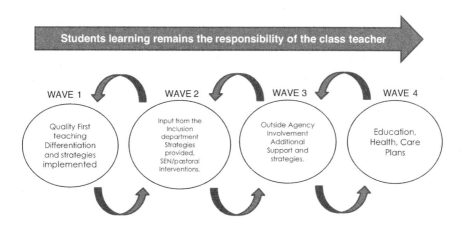

This statement from the DfE, 2015 is a crucial one and one that should underpin this diagram and your strategic leadership of the teaching and learning side of SEND:

> Special educational provision is underpinned by high quality teaching and is compromised by anything less.

When discussing 'Learning without Limits', this quote is an effective starting point to highlight how it affects Wave One.

Wave One – quality-first teaching

This is your driver, your ethos, your values and, most importantly, where you invest professional development and training time for the staff. Train them in the needs of your children, give them the skills and the confidence to deliver Wave One, and the staff and the children will flourish.

A lot has been said and written about *quality-first teaching* in recent times due to its heightened focus within the Code of Practice. As educators we want all of our lessons to be excellent, and all of our children to enjoy their learning. It is why we do what we do. In order to support a quality-first teaching provision, it is crucial you remove as many barriers to success as you can. You must ensure that the way your team communicates is beneficial for staff and supports the work they do day in and day out. From a SEND perspective it is about ensuring that you communicate the needs of the pupils in a sensible, transparent and jargon-free way.

Think about the following questions.

- How will you as a leader of inclusion communicate these needs?

- What are the specific difficulties that the children face?

Break this down further – there is no point just putting 'Moderate Learning Difficulty' on the information. What does that mean for that child?

- What does that mean for the member of staff teaching them?

- What strategies can teachers employ to support the child's learning?

Case study

The SENDCO and I made sure that our one-page profiles were succinct and focused on the strategies that staff could use in the classroom rather the pupil's difficulties. One pupil in question found focusing in class difficult. This led to being distracted and distracting, and would result in them escalating through the behaviour system. We gave the staff five key strategies to use in the lesson at different stages.

Start of the lesson

1 To give the pupil a job. This would be giving books or work out, and help to give them responsibility.

2 To have two short, sharp recap tasks on a sheet of paper ready for them to start on straight away.

3 Seating plan – they were to sit close to the teacher at the front to offer support.

Main part of the lesson

Each lesson had a period of time where pupils were expected to work hard and in silence for at least 15 minutes. The strategy here was to ask staff to break the task down into sections for the pupil to achieve and to use a bookmark guide (4) to indicate the length of writing to keep them focused. (5) We asked staff to check in on them every couple of minutes and 'live mark' their work to keep them motivated.

End of lesson

We gave the pupil a positive progress report and asked staff to add two things they did well in the lesson to finish with a positive.

These strategies led to the pupil having a significant reduction in the number of behaviour incidents they accrued, and they had a much more positive view of lessons, and therefore improved confidence. They started making more progress. This work was successful due to its personal nature and being really clear and prescriptive with the strategies for staff.

One-page profiles/ILPs/IEPs

To achieve quality-first teaching in every class, we must support our colleagues to facilitate this. This is done through sharing key information and giving clarity, followed by training them well.

The SENDCO will ensure that they produce information about children's needs and share these with staff. Your school may call these pieces of information different names. They could be a *one-page profile,* an *Individual Learning Plan (ILP)* or an *Individual Education Plan (IEP).* It is the information that they hold that is the key to unlocking children's potential. They should have the following on them:

- Identified SEN need
- Their strengths
- Their weaknesses
- What they enjoy
- What they dislike
- What strategies staff can use to support them

Review these and communicate with the staff.

- What do they find useful in them?
- Which bits?
- Do they not find them useful? Why?

IEPs can become long, too detailed and too confusing. If you are producing these for all pupils on your SEN register, there is a lot of reading and interpreting for staff. Make sure they support quality-first teaching and inform pedagogy; ask your SENDCO to quality assure their use and to check pupils are getting the support they need.

Teaching and learning, and the curriculum, underpin this work. While this is not the area of senior leadership I am focusing on, you must have some input into these areas and ensure that the needs of children are met within them. Work closely with the senior colleagues responsible for each area, and determine what an inclusive curriculum looks like and that children's learning needs are met routinely in the classroom. Quality-first teaching will only bring about success for the children if you have a curriculum that is fit for purpose and meets children's needs. We get bogged down with the term *differentiation* and, if we are not careful, we can mesmerise staff with the variety of differentiation methods out there. SEND shouldn't mean that we lower our expectations. Make sure staff have sky high expectations for all learners.

Stretch and scaffold

The best way to support pupils and differentiate is to *teach to the top*.

Tom Sherrington (2017), in his book *The Learning Rainforest*, promotes this idea by stating:

> It's a win-win to cater explicitly for the highest attaining students in any group; to 'teach to the top', pitching every lesson and the general thrust of every unit of work to stretch them. In doing so, everyone benefits.

We must not lower our expectations for pupils with SEND. We raise the bar and push everyone to be the best they can be and then scaffold any of the learning down to those that need it.

Use your TAs to offer group or individual support, or use them to teach the class while your teachers offer some 1:1 teaching that skills up the children that need it. Make sure you have your finger on the pulse in the teaching and learning in your school. We know that curriculum models won't change that much and, in a time where budgets are tight, curriculum-led financial planning is the head teacher's best friend, but you can still influence what is being taught and how.

For example:

- What do department curriculum plans look like?
- How do they accommodate the needs of all?
- How does the assessment calendar and process identify areas of need?
- Is your assessment process robust and accurate?
- How do department leads, pastoral leads, the SENDCO and you utilise this data to target intervention?

A consistent lesson cycle can really support the needs of SEND pupils. They get used to the structure and they have the chance to embed learning. Using retrieval and deliberate practice can facilitate this learning. Rosenshine's *Principles of Instruction* (2012) gave clear research evidence of the importance of using these 'principles'.

In 'Teaching Walkthrus' (Sherrington and Caviglioli, 2020), focus is placed on the scaffolding for difficult tasks. It emphasises the need for this approach but also that 'scaffolding is only temporary and must not become relied upon'. We have to build resilience in our SEND learners too. Despite our best endeavours to meet all pupils' needs in the classroom, there are times when Wave One simply isn't enough, and we must engage in a graduated response to meet children's needs.

Learning without Limits – a graduated response to inclusion

We know that pupils will fall behind or need support in one or a multitude of the SEND areas of need. We also know that generally speaking, some of these needs land on the pastoral team's door as 'behaviour'. This is what triggers our inclusion graduated response. Figure 3.1 is a document that was developed by a group of senior leaders across Rotherham as part of process to access more school-to-support and provision for those that need it. This document can really help to focus the work of your pastoral and SEND teams and it is the starting point of creating a timeline of evidence for supporting a pupil's needs. It is important that you build up an evidence base of support at each wave to contribute to further assessment for EHCPs.

Graduated response sheet

You can add whatever heading you want in each phase/wave, but these have to match up to what you can offer within your school. Our pastoral leads keep these as live documents and add dates, meetings, actions and impact as we go through the year. The bottom section is for Phase/Wave Three, where you can identify your external partners and processes. This is where you are moving towards an EHCP assessment and further specialist support. I also ask my team to use the bottom boxes to add any safeguarding or other relevant information.

These forms are used for children who may be falling behind in lessons and learning, or which children are becoming your big hitters in terms of poor behaviour. There shouldn't be too many of these forms being used in each year group. The latest data indicates that there are 3.1% of children who have an EHCP in the entire country – more justification to ensure that you target detailed graduated responses at the small percentage of children who need it. As each child receives more support, they will be moving through the waves and getting extra intervention. It is crucial that you measure the impact. If an intervention has had no impact, then you must

Graduated Response to SEMH needs

Name

What are we worried about? (Total amount)			
Attendance		On-call count	
Late Marks		SLT detentions	
Behaviour Points		IE days total	
Detentions		FTE days total	

Phase 1

Intervention	Date	By Whom	Impact
Department Report			
Form tutor			
HOY report - green			
Class Change/half of year move			
Time out card			
Use of IEP strategies			
Fidget Toys/sensory breaks			
Change of seating plan			
Supported social times			
Use of restorative practice and emotional coaching			
1:1 support via SWM/SAL			
Regular check-ins			

Phase 2

Intervention	Date	By Whom	Impact
Form Tutor Report			
HOY Report – yellow/red			
Behaviour contract			
REACH referral			
Individual Reward System			
Form/Change in Timetable			
MAST referral			
Early Help referral			
SEN referral			
Referral to other outside agencies			
Multi-agency Meeting/Support			
Respite at another school			
SEN support plan			
IEP			
SALT referral			
Boxall			
Trailblazer			

Phase 3

Intervention	Date	By Whom	Impact
PSP			
Educational Psychologist – consultation			
Educational Psychologist – full referral			
Alternative Provision			
Managed move via Trust			
Discussed at Partnership Group			
Managed Move			

Ensure all evidence is attached to this document.

Other relevant comments (safeguarding/context)	Date/Impact

Figure 3.1 An example of a graduated response

leave it and try something else. These forms and the work you do in each phase/wave will determine what your inclusive offer looks like, but it will also allow you as the leader to identify gaps in your provision and then to plan to plug them.

Wave Two – the intervention wave for inclusion

Wave Two is when the basic daily work of your pastoral leads, form tutor and other staff hasn't had the desired effect. You need to build up a provision that meets the more complex needs of children and where you can utilise testing packages or assessment tools. Things like Boxall profiling, SALT referrals, access arrangement testing, counselling and other interventions really help your work. You need to look at some external support here and the strategies they give. You also need to have internal provisions that can support you. These require staffing, a physical space and money, so make sure you have your long-term plans and impact statements ready when you meet with the head teacher to discuss setting up things like this.

In order to signpost our children to these provisions, we meet as a team on a weekly basis which I call our *interventions meeting*. Here heads of year bring children from their groups who need more support or intervention, and they discuss what was already put in place at Wave One. The SENDCO or assistant SENDCO attend so we can triangulate interventions, resulting in either therapeutic or social, emotional and mental health (SEMH) support being assigned. It is really important that these meetings are held. They give you oversight of what is happening, they allow you to encourage and empower others to contribute and make decisions but, also, they bring you closer together as a team.

What follows are examples that have been successful in the inclusion teams I have led.

Wave Two provisions

Hub

A Hub is usually part of the SEND area and is where small group or 1:1 intervention takes place. It is also used as a safe space for pupils who may need it. Pupils meet their key workers there and may also be occasionally taught here. Things like breakfast clubs and after school homework clubs are also run from here. It is strategically led by the SENDCO and operates as a confidence boosting area where pupils with SEND needs can learn and visit when required. You may also, if the budget allows, have a Hub manager.

REACH

This is a provision used in my current setting, staffed by a REACH leader and another colleague who is a qualified teacher. This provision is a SEMH provision that supports the needs of pupils who may be displaying challenging behaviours or who are unable to regulate their emotions.

REACH stands for **Raising Engagement Attainment Communication and Health**. Pupils can be referred to this provision by pastoral leaders, and they need to bring the child's graduated response and information to discuss why they need to access REACH and for how long. Pupils can access REACH full or part time. In REACH a pupil gets therapeutic support for their emotional needs and is also taught curriculum content. The therapy gives the pupil strategies to use back in the mainstream, and the teacher then ensures they don't fall any farther behind. You must also remember to reinforce to your teaching staff that if a pupil is in REACH rather than their lesson, they are still accountable for delivering resources to be taught and they are accountable for their progress. What you offer here, and the staffing and interventions, depends on the budget and the skill set of your staff.

Bridge

The Bridge is a provision used by many schools. It's a provision that supports the needs of our more vulnerable children. The idea was that the provision was to support pupils who:

- Needed a boost of confidence
- Needed to break a negative cycle
- Needed an area to study while recovering from an illness or serious injury
- Needed gradual re-integration into the school as they had just moved into the area or back into mainstream provision

Our children came from very disadvantaged backgrounds and, therefore, we knew we needed to invest heavily in inclusion to ensure we had enough wrap-around support in place. Any spare staffing was used in the Bridge. Colleagues would be timetabled in the area and would deliver either small group or 1:1 support in their specialism. The job description of our second in faculties required them to ensure the Bridge had enough appropriate work for all year groups and it was assessed and marked so pupils still made progress while there.

Ethos and Engagement (this was the name of our provision)

This was our internal alternative provision that was created at one of my previous schools. We invested heavily in inclusion as we felt that our children would need this support, and there were very few alternative provisions that we felt were (a) any good, (b) gave value for money and (c) gave the pupil something they could use for the next stage of their education. It was primarily for Year 11 pupils who were disengaged with school and were on a path of exclusion and poor behaviour.

We tailored the provision to meet their needs more, and with a smaller group, more support and less pressure, they felt more supported. We had pupils who still achieved 5A*-C including English and maths. It was located within the school, and we had a curriculum offer drawn up for these children, including the core subjects plus a selection of other subjects we could deliver. Two full-time TAs were timetabled to work within it as the children needed a high level of support. Staff also taught their specialism in there. Pupils came in at a normal time, registered in there and had their break and lunch in the area. It was a highly successful intervention that meant pupils could continue at our school and get some form of outcomes at the end. The downside was the cost, and when you run a provision like this in Year 11 there is always a negative impact on headline figures. During numerous OFSTED inspections, all our provisions and our ethos behind them was praised.

Athena

Athena's primary purpose was to support pupils who didn't meet age-related expectations at Key Stage 2 and to allow them to close the gap on their peers. The strapline for Athena was 'A primary based provision with secondary based expectations'.

The children were identified at transition and had scored in the mid or low 80s in their scalded score from Key Stage 2. The main issue was that their literacy skills were very underdeveloped. They were taught every day within Athena. A thematic curriculum was planned and delivered, and we appointed a primary trained SENDCO to lead the provision and deliver most of the teaching. She went back to basics with some of the students as that was what they needed; reading ages were very low and the pupils' understanding of literacy was way behind. She assessed their progress and when she felt they had closed the gap, they 'graduated' into the mainstream. The provision was line managed by an assistant principal who was also the English faculty lead. She ensured standards were sky high and literacy was a key focus. They still could touch base with the provision and had support in lessons until they were fully integrated. The results were amazing. Reading, writing and arithmetic skills were rapidly improved, their confidence was high, and we even had one pupil who was a selective mute begin to converse with others on a daily basis. Some of the pupils in there stayed within the provision, and may indeed stay in there for the full five years if that is what is appropriate and necessary to get them what they need and for them to have a successful school life. We had to ensure that the funds were available in the budget and had to staff the provision as part of our financial planning document. Some of the funding for pupil premium and SEND was used to support the cost of running the provision.

One success story I remember was one boy who joined us in Year 7 as an in-year admission who came from Romania. He spoke very little English at first and we had no prior data or any understanding of his needs. He really excelled in Athena and brought his skills up to where they needed to be. He developed friendships that he may not have had in the mainstream and Athena developed his confidence and skill set. He transitioned into mainstream provision and began making progress in line with his peers.

Athena was given the external recognition it deserved when the school was part of a two-day external visit by Challenge Partners. It was highlighted as an 'Area of Excellence' and was to be shared with other Challenge Partner schools as a beacon of excellent practice. Those staff thoroughly deserved that.

Thinking point two

- What provisions at Wave Two does your current setting have?
- Does each one meet the needs of your children? How do you know?
- If you could create a provision to support the needs of your children in your setting, where money wasn't a barrier, what would this be?
- What would it look like?

This is a perfect chance for some blue-sky thinking – jot down your ideas.

Wave Three – the final support mechanism

The final stage of our graduated response to discuss is Wave Three. This relates to external support and how you access that. Many of you as pastoral leads may already be involved in different school-to-school support groups. As a pastoral lead you will need to bring evidence to these meetings that shows you have put a graduated response in place for your pupil, tried everything to support them and that you are now requesting further support that could lead to a managed move. Each Local Authority will have a different procedure and protocol around managed moves, but when done correctly with open dialogue and professional challenge, these types of Wave Three intervention can really support the pupil in getting a fresh start and some success.

Most of the work at Wave Three will be done by your SENDCO. They will refer to educational psychologists to get external, expert opinions on a child. The SENDCO will also fill in all the necessary paperwork for an EHCP assessment. These assessments and the paperwork associated will vary from each authority. As a leader of inclusion, you just need to be aware of the Assess, Plan, Do, Review (APDR) cycle and that your SENDCO has put a plan in place that evidences this. It may be useful when you have your line management or triangulation meetings to ask to see a SEND support plan and the evidence of the APDR cycle. There really should be at least three cycles before you start to think about an assessment for an EHCP.

Good professional development for you as the inclusion lead would be to sit with your SENDCO when they write an APDR cycle, see how they set the targets for the child and how they gather their evidence. Then ask to see an EHCP assessment and familiarise yourself with what is required and the level of detail needed.

Educational provisions are expected to document two terms for APDR cycles to get substantial evidence to support a child moving towards an EHCP.

Social, emotional and mental health difficulties

I want to end the chapter with one of the most overlooked and least understood areas of SEND. This can be the main type of SEND need that you will come across, not necessarily at the EHCP level but certainly at the SEND support level.

SEMH needs are certainly becoming more prevalent in the last few years in today's society. Poor parenting, drug abuse, alcoholism, computer games and lack of playing outside may all have an impact on a child's mental health, and I throw our current education system in there as well. While writing this book we have all had to deal with the impact of COVID-19, and I'm sure we will be supporting children from the fallout of this for a while to come.

SEMH support

There are numerous books that you can read and ample research into what impacts on our mental health. I would like to give a snapshot of two main contributors that I come across every day. I want to talk a little about these and look at what you as a senior leader of inclusion can do to support children.

Trauma at any age, but particularly in childhood, is one of the biggest factors in children developing a SEMH need. Karen Odenko, in her 'What is Trauma' article via integrated listening (https://integratedlistening.com/what-is-trauma/), defines trauma as:

> the response to a deeply distressing or disturbing event that overwhelms an individual's ability to cope, causing feelings of helplessness, diminishes their sense of self and their ability to feel the full range of emotions and experiences.

Lots of our children will have experienced trauma, and reading that quote I can already see lots of children who I have supported over the years. Our children will experience a variety of traumas that range from family deaths to divorce of their parents. Witnessing domestic violence and injury will have a longer lasting effect, as will any form of abuse. How many of your children are you aware of that have witnessed these things? How did these alter their behaviour? What did you do? What did you tell the staff?

Some of the symptoms and responses we could see based on a child experiencing trauma could be:

- Sadness
- Anger
- Denial
- Fear
- Shame

These primary symptoms can lead then to more complications such as nightmares and emotional outbursts. The long-term effects of trauma can lead to depression and anxiety. This is where knowing your children and their families can really help. In your role you will either be the Designated Safeguarding Lead or a deputy, so you will be privy to this information. I will cover safeguarding in a later chapter, but it's important that you use the information you can access in this role to support your children. Make sure you know everything about the children who are on a child protection plan, who are subject to child in need or who have an Early Help Assessment in place. Make sure you are also aware of your Looked After Children (LAC) and what difficulties/experiences they have had. These will be much more complex and need much more wrap-around care, hence the pupil premium plus funding that they can access. As a senior leader of inclusion, you have a duty of care to these children to inform staff that they have had significant trauma in their lives and how this may make them behave in their class. You do not need to break any confidentiality or discuss the finer details, but you can inform staff how they may feel in certain situations and how staff can best de-escalate situations or support any emotional outbursts.

Adverse Childhood Experiences (ACEs)

Closely related to trauma is a term that is being used quite a lot by mental health practitioners, educational psychologists and other professionals: Adverse Childhood Experiences (ACEs). Research indicates that the more ACEs a child suffers from, then the more likely they will experience poor health in the future and there is also a strong correlation with poor academic achievement. These ACEs and other negative influences that a child may experience in their community, when combined with a lack of adult support, can lead to toxic stress. Toxic stress is a term that is used to describe effects of the child's stress response system being constantly fired. The key information to take from this, though, is that a child who has experienced many ACEs and toxic stress in their lives is not irreparably damaged and we can support these children in our settings.

- Reduce stress – we can try and make school life less stressful by offering more support and listening. If the stressors are at home, then this is where key work around Early Help Assessments and the right external agency to support the family are crucial.

- Provide responsive relationships – this goes back to the ethos of the school and what drives the adults. We need adults in our schools, and especially in our teams, that can empathise, and can show love, compassion and care. This is where a skilled pastoral team can have real impact.

- Strengthen core life skills – our curriculum content can help here in how we teach children about the skills needed in life through areas such as PSHE. We can also build resilience and determination by offering safe challenges. Simple things like house competitions, sports days, countdown assemblies and spelling bees can all help.

We also need to offer specialist support within our schools and our inclusion team structure so we can meet some of the acute needs that may be displayed.

This comes back to you as the senior leader for inclusion.

- What does your structure look like?
- Where are your gaps?
- How will you fund extra interventions and staff?

SEMH case studies

Dramatherapy

You have to see the bigger picture and make sure you have the right team of people with the right skill set around you. In a previous setting, we had quite a few LAC and we were finding it difficult to meet some of their emotional needs due to the level of childhood trauma they had faced. I used their Electronic Personal Education Plans (EPEPs) and pupil premium plus funding to source a drama therapist who came and worked with them once a week on a 1:1 basis to give them specialist therapeutic support. It worked really well. The children began to open up and had less emotional outbursts, and it allowed the therapist to offer some excellent strategies for the children and our staff – think outside the box sometimes.

Counselling

In our current setting we employ two full-time counsellors that we can refer children to for a piece of therapeutic work based on improving their mental health needs. Again, this is something you have to cost and present an argument for, but if your children need it then it is your job to get it in place. This level of support is just as important as having an excellent teacher in front of the children. This therapeutic work is going to be needed even more over the coming years. Pupils are working in schools where there is a culture of testing, exams and pressure. This only builds up over time and we need to make sure we have the right level of support for our children.

To finish this chapter on SEND, I want to highlight the key skills and attributes that a senior leader of inclusion should work towards when focusing on SEND as a takeaway section for you.

The best senior leaders on inclusion have an:

- Understanding that a diagnosis is just the label – it is the support around the holistic child that has the impact. This support ultimately comes from the school.

- Understanding that these children will not necessarily impact positively on the outcomes of the school, but the small steps they make are rewarding for families and key workers (get your SENDCO to be able to show these).

- Understanding that the SEN register is a report and an understanding of the importance of knowing these students. This should be reflective of the journey the pupils have had. Make sure you know this document.

- Understanding that relationships with external agencies, families and the SENDCO are paramount.

Leading inclusion scenario three

You arrive at a school as inclusion lead. In your first meeting with the head teacher, you discuss that the school has a deficit of over 300 EHCP hours and there are limited graduated support strategies. When looking at the SEN cohort, there is a large proportion of SEN pupils on partial timetables and a number of SEN pupils with no support packages (EHCPs, SEN support plans) as school refusers and a deficit of Year 11 outcomes of -1.29 for the SEND cohort. What follows is a reflection on this chapter and your leadership of SEND. Prioritise your short-term strategies and plan long-term impact.

- What would you tackle first? Think about the impact of partial timetables on a child and their learning.

- Think about how you communicate pupils' needs to staff.

- How do you as a school quality assure teaching and learning? Could this help you?

- What interventions could you design that could help to close attainment and progress gaps, and what skills would you look at?

Chapter 3 references and research

Department for Education (DfE). (2015). *Special Educational Needs and Disability Code of Practice: 0 to 25 Years Statutory Guidance for Organisations Which Work With and Support Children and Young People Who Have Special Educational Needs or Disabilities.* https://www.gov.uk/government/publications/send-code-of-practice-0-to-25

Rosenshine, B. (2012, Spring). Principles of Instruction: Research-Based Strategies That All Teachers Should Know. *American Educator,* 36(1), 12-39.

Sherrington, T. (2017). *The Learning Rainforest. Great Teaching in Real Classrooms.* Jon Catt Educational Limited.

Sherrington, T., and Caviglioli, O. (2020). *Teaching Walkthrus. Five Step Guides to Instructional Coaching.* Jon Catt Educational Limited.

Systems, systems, systems
Developing, embedding and measuring

This chapter's focus is all about the systems that you will need to rely on for you to do your job. Efficient systems will support you and make your teams work. Clunky, complicated systems will hinder you. The chapter looks at the behaviour systems you will come to rely on in your role and suggests a few methods you could use to change pupil behaviour. The chapter emphasises the need to develop, embed and measure your systems. We will discuss behaviour systems, detentions and how you can get pupils to reflect on their behaviour. The chapter finishes with a look at rewards and how to ensure the balance is more in favour of positive reinforcement than negative. As you move through the chapter, reflect fully on what your views on behaviour are and how you want your ethos from our earlier chapter to influence this. This thought process will help you formulate an argument for the scenario at the end.

Setting up and implementing an effective behaviour system

> Ambiguity is great for certain kinds of creative activities, but it is the mortal enemy of systems design.
>
> (Stephen Haeckel)

Any system you introduce into a school setting has to be clear, simple and purposeful. The moment there is any ambiguity or confusion, the system fails as the staff and the children will exploit it. Have this clear in your head when you are reviewing or implementing behaviour systems within your school. If you are going to be successful in your role, have strategic oversight and ensure staff and children are supported, then you need effective systems. Most behaviour systems now originate with some form of increasing tariff. These will be noted and visible in classrooms, in policies and on websites. The main work of the system, though, tends to be through an IT-based reporting mechanism that can collate trends and key figures for you. When you are in your developing stage, think what IT system you may need to support your work in the embedding and measuring stage. A well-written app or spreadsheet will save you time and produce key data at the drop of a hat.

Developing the system

Firstly, what do we mean by an effective system?

- What should it look like?

- What should it contain?

The answers to these questions will depend largely upon your setting, especially how pupils behave, and you also need to remember that there may already be a trust approach that you have to use.

A system defined in the Oxford Dictionary is:

> a set of principles or procedures according to which something is done; an organised scheme or method.

Key words to take out of this quote when planning or reviewing your behaviour systems are *set of principles* and *organised*. Remember that your behaviour policy is your start point for your behaviour system, and every member of staff is bound by their contract to follow policy. Your system should be an integral part of your policy and it needs to be organised. Your colleagues need a system that is easy to follow, implement and report upon.

Reflect back to your days as a main scale teacher, teaching maybe four or five lessons every day, if you were lucky, in the same classroom. Your colleagues need simple, effective and supportive systems so they can report any issues easily and quickly. There are lots of systems out there that can help with this and they allow you to tailor them to the needs of your school; research which are best for you. I have seen creative systems on SIMS, seen schools design their own via Google forms and some schools make use of external partners via a service level agreement.

My systems

When designing and implementing a system, try and involve the staff along the way, perhaps by utilising a working group. Make sure you use staff to evaluate and review the system when it starts and make small changes along the way, when required. I like to embed best practice in the classroom first. I operate a system with three to five classroom rules and expectations that children and staff can follow.

These are simple and to the point:

- Equipment out and ready to learn

- Follow staff instructions – first time, every time

- Do not disrupt the learning of others

- Listen when others are talking

If they break one of those rules, they are warned. They get three warnings; everyone makes mistakes and we have to give children the chance to recognise a mistake and be responsible for changing their own behaviour and making correct choices. In our system, after three warnings a child will be removed from learning if they get it wrong again. Some people will argue that they should only get one chance and that four mistakes is too many times that learning can be disrupted. My ethos is predicated around allowing children to see they've made a mistake and then to correct it. Education is not limited, and modelling and sharing how to emotionally regulate is embedded through practice.

- How many times have you made a mistake as an adult?

- Did your colleague or family member ban you from the room or their house?

No, they speak to you about it and you realise what you've done and learn from it. We have to remember we are working with precious lives. These are children, and our job is to educate them, which involves behaviour expectations as well. Some of them are coming from family lives where they don't have positive role models or the chance to learn from mistakes. One of my most important values to be driven through my systems is that staff need to **model behaviour**.

Staff use our system to log warnings without any detail, unless a child has to be removed from class. This is where I ask staff to write more detail and to call home to parents. It is vital that colleagues hold regular conversations with parents about good and bad experiences in the classroom, and 99% of the time parents are very supportive. If a child is removed from a lesson, we operate a system of 'on-call' and a senior leader, pastoral leader or middle leader will be on duty and will take the pupil to another lesson in the department. The teacher sends the work with the child and they work in another room within the department. This also emphasises the middle leadership aspect of behaviour management. At the end of the lesson, they take their work back and have a conversation with their teacher to try and 'restore' the situation. The child is given a same day 30-minute detention. This may or may not work in your setting and that is fine. You need to have a system that works for you, your staff and your children. Make sure that your system is tiered and that it is clearly indicated what behaviour leads to what consequence. My current one is shown in Figure 4.1; for our children and staff who are consistently using it each day, it is clear and uncomplicated.

Thinking point one

Reflect on the schools you have worked in since you became a newly qualified teacher (NQT) or started your pastoral or associate staff role.

- What systems were in place for monitoring and reporting behaviour?

- Did they work?

- What was useful to you as the teacher?

- What didn't work and why?

Jot down your thoughts and how you might have developed these differently.

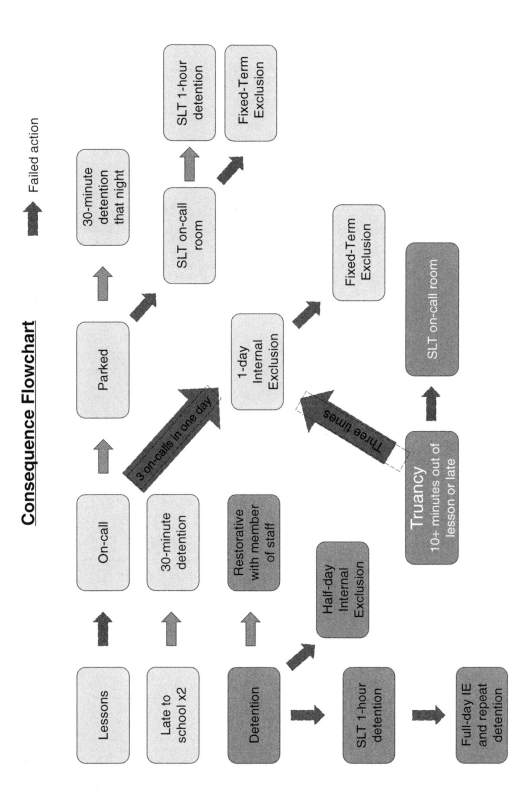

Figure 4.1 Example of consequence flowchart

Embedding the system

Consequence tiers

Whatever school setting you work in, there will be tiered consequences. This is normal and helps children to understand that different behaviour choices can lead to different consequences. The difficulty, though, is determining what behaviour requires what consequence and ensuring there is **consistency** in its application. The first level of any tiered system is usually detentions, and it is really important that the process for giving detentions is clear and that the children understand what they are for. There will be some other behaviours and incidents that require more than a detention. This is where you rely on your team to fully investigate what happened and get a clear picture of what occurred.

- What are your systems for reporting and recording these incidents?
- Do they need to be approved by you, as the pastoral lead?
- Remember to refer back to the SEND chapter – have they got an underlying condition?
- Did something trigger their behaviour?

Once you have this information, then you can start to make decisions and it is important to treat each case and each consequence on an individual basis. This is where prescriptive consequence ladders can cause issues, and you need to use your evidence and experience to decide what the outcome will be and not necessarily a table.

There are several common consequences that appear in every school. I am going to discuss a few of these, and hopefully stir up some debate and feelings as you read this. There is no right or wrong. Colleagues in our profession and in a pastoral role are trying to do the best for their children. Some consequences will work for some, but not others. Use what is best for your children and your setting and always remember to stand by those values of yours!

Detentions

Detentions don't change behaviour. They can be used as an effective consequence, but they will not change behaviour as most of them are not part of what Dreikurs and Grey (1993) termed 'logical or natural consequences'. Natural consequences occur as a result of a presented behaviour. For example, if a child goes out at break time in the rain without a coat, they will be wet and cold for the rest of the day. A natural consequence allows a child to experience the unpleasantness of their behaviour and learn from it.

Logical consequences

A logical consequence will be designed by an adult in advance of a behaviour occurring. For example, a child drops litter; the logical consequence is they pick it up when asked. The adult then has a conversation about why they should put it in a bin and not drop the litter. A detention is not necessarily a logical consequence. If a child gets removed from a lesson at 9:30 a.m. and placed in detention later that day in a room with a different adult and is given a meaningless task, their behaviour is unlikely to change. If the detention is held at the end of the lesson and the teacher speaks to the pupil about their behaviour and what they can both do differently next time, it becomes more logical to the child. This can, however, be difficult to do during a busy day and it might not work during lesson changeovers.

One way you can try and make the detention more logical to the child is to ask the member of staff who gave the detention to attend it and talk to the pupil. Cotton (2010) demonstrated that educating young people through consequences is more effective than the use of punishments. Some settings will also ask pupils to use detention time to complete academic tasks and improve their skills. Smith (2005) concluded that this approach didn't improve behaviour because it did not address the behaviours that the children had exhibited to get the detention in the first place.

Centralised detentions

Many detention systems are centralised, either every day or some days. They are a deterrent mainly to other children to avoid behaving in a way that warrants a detention, but they do not change behaviour. Settings will also use centralised detentions to support the work-life balance of their staff. However, if you are going to change behaviour of children and support staff in dealing with this, then you have to empower the staff to tackle the behaviour. A centralised system does not allow this to happen and it can, in a way, send an indirect message that as a senior leader you are not bothered about how children behave in lessons; you will pick up the pieces. Instead you want staff that are confident, skilled and supported when dealing with behaviour. They have a professional responsibility to 'teach' good behaviour, so you must allow that to happen. We currently do this by asking staff to come to a detention and have a restorative conversation with children. You, again, may disagree with me here, but I firmly believe that staff have been seriously de-skilled in managing behaviour since the invention of C-coded systems, remove rooms and centralised detentions.

Post-incident learning (PIL)

One way that I tried to have a system that fits the needs of staff and pupils with detentions was to create a 'post-incident learning sheet'. Dean Cotton's research (2013) looked at the impact of detention on changing behaviour and whether a post-incident discussion with a child would help to change their behaviour. He developed a

PIL app which can be found in the Google and Apple app stores and is great to use. Cotton completed a design research study with our children and looked at how reflective conversations with staff via the app could change behaviour. The conclusion of Cotton's work with our children was that there was a 65% reduction in behaviour incidents from the target groups in a three-month period when using the PIL.

This powerful and meaningful research demonstrated to me that we had to start speaking to children and discussing the incidents that occurred in our classrooms and school. I tweaked it a little. It can be used in all settings; you ask the child to complete the form and reflect on their behaviour. The form goes back to the teacher to inform a discussion about their behaviour and how to change it.

The PIL sheet is shown here:

Post-Incident Learning
Name: _____

What made you behave the way you did?

How did it make you feel?

What will you do differently next time you feel like that?

Children find it difficult to explain behaviours or situations they find themselves in. They do understand feelings. The first question tries to get them to explain what happened, then to ask how it made them feel and finally if they feel that way again, what they can do differently. This allows the child to reflect, allows you to find out

> **Post Incident Learning - Ask these questions**
>
> 1) What made you behave the way you did?
> 2) How did it make you feel?
> 3) What can you do the next time you feel like that?
> 4) How can you begin to put things right from next lesson?

Figure 4.2

what occurred and also to start to unpick feelings. From these conversations we had feelings such as angry, sad, anxious, embarrassed and stupid identified by the children. As adults, when we feel those ways we behave differently, so why would children be any different? It, then, allowed us to unpick the situations, add support and communicate with the class teacher.

I also produced little laminated cards like the ones in Figure 4.2 to help staff to ask these questions too.

Thinking point two

- Do detentions work?
- As a member of staff, do detentions support you?
- Does the centralised detention system help to improve behaviour of pupils in your class?
- Do you feel behaviour in your lesson is your responsibility or should disruptive children be removed and dealt with by leaders? Why?

Jot down your views on these points.

The outcomes of your system

Remove room

In the last decade these rooms will have been seen in most secondary settings. If a school runs a warning system, then at some stage a child will be removed from the lesson and taken here. This sprang up so that schools could minimise low-level disruption affecting other learners in class. Don't get me wrong, there are ways this is done both correctly and incorrectly, but we also must ensure that teachers are given the chance to teach and that children can learn without disruption. The key is how you support children who are disruptive and to unpick where this behaviour is coming from. A remove room in some settings is a necessary evil. It's an evil as such, as the child being removed loses their learning and this is where your system needs to pick this up and spot any trends, and then support the child. If a child is constantly removed from learning, can you find out why?

- Is it a learning need?
- Anxiety?

- Saving face?

- Poor relationships?

It is our job to find out and put support in place. I have had remove rooms in the schools I have worked in, including an outstanding secondary mainstream, but I have moved away from them. I prefer a parking system where staff work with each other and the children to support changes in behaviour. The remove room will not change behaviour and it creates other problematic issues for you to manage. When I did use them, I tried to use the PIL sheets to unpick what had happened and find a way to move forward. Reflect on your setting again, though. There may be a time where you need this kind of provision and it may help for a time, but don't be scared to take it away.

Parking

Instead of placing children in a remove room, I prefer to use a system where you call upon the middle leaders of the school to support the behaviour system. Middle leaders have ownership of their department, the work, the standards and the outcomes, and therefore should also have ownership of behaviour. This system allows them to identify rooms within their department where the child can be parked if they are removed from their classroom. The child takes their book and their work with them. At the end they take their book back and when possible have a restorative conversation with the teacher.

This process allows the head of department to have oversight of challenging classes or pupils, and to support members of their team. It also allows the child who has been removed the chance to carry on with their work and have another specialist on hand to support them. Your behaviour reporting system should identify where there may be consistent removes and you can then ensure your pastoral team or head of department is on hand to go into these lessons. We call them *hotspots*. In my experience, both teaching staff and heads of department welcome this approach and the middle leaders certainly enjoy stepping up and managing their area.

Internal exclusion

This system is widely used and can be an effective way to manage levels of more challenging behaviour, and also to prevent a fixed term exclusion. Sometimes it is not appropriate to use a fixed-term exclusion, as it may put the child at more harm and also it may not be the way to make them reflect on and change their behaviour. An internal exclusion room is generally staffed by a full-time member of staff, with support from senior leaders; their layouts and processes will differ. Some are more punitive and rigid; others are more open and reflective. Each school will decide the best way for themselves. The most common approach is to use booths where children sit, complete their work in silence and do not leave their area. I don't want to get into a #banthebooths argument as I believe, if used correctly, a booth can be an effective way to support a child and help them to reflect on their behaviour. However, prolonged use will have a negative effect on a child's mental health. If you are using a booth consistently with the same child for long periods, then you are not tackling the issue or supporting their development. There are some specialist settings I know that use booths to support their complex learners – it's about how you use them, what they are for and what the children see them as. I prefer an open layout that is classroom based, where children can work in silence but reflect on their behaviour.

To have an effective internal exclusion, you need an effective system behind it. Think about these questions.

- Who has day-to-day oversight and responsibility for it?

- Who can and can't place children in there?

- What are the behaviours or events that would result in an internal exclusion – are these shared? Are they part of your behaviour consequence system?

- What work will the children do in there? We have a reflection sheet for the first ten minutes where the children discuss the event that occurred and how they could handle it differently. We then have a report card for each child, and they set targets for the day. We reward good work and effort via this card, and report back to parents at the end of the day.

- Do you have different start and finish times for the internal exclusion? A longer day may result in pupils seeing it as a more punitive consequence – it is about getting the balance right.

- How do you ensure teaching staff set the appropriate work for children in there?

- How do you communicate this to staff?

- How early do you let staff who are planning lessons know that (a) the pupil won't be in their lesson and (b) that you need some work?

- Children most definitely need a break and toilet breaks while in the room – how do you manage this? How do you get food orders? When is their lunchtime?

- How do you meet the needs of SEN pupils in this system?

- Are you aware you could be setting up a child to fail by using this consequence?

- How do you mitigate against that, while ensuring there is an appropriate consequence for their behaviour?

An effective room is only effective when all these questions are answered, the system is smooth and you see fewer and fewer repeat offenders.

Fixed-term exclusion

A fixed-term exclusion is a vital part of a behaviour management system. It is your job as inclusion lead to ensure that you and your team have investigated all the events and taken all statements before requesting an exclusion from the principal. The principal is the only person who can issue a fixed-term exclusion, so you must ensure you have all the evidence you need. The Department for Education (2017) guidance *Exclusion from Maintained Schools, Academies and Pupil Referral Units* indicates that you do not have to have a return from exclusion meeting and some parents will avoid these – make sure you can hold as many of these as you can. These meetings help to discuss the issues and the next steps and to hold both the pupil and parents accountable for behaviour.

I know of settings that avoid giving fixed-term exclusions so their figures aren't scrutinised by external agencies. They also don't use repeated exclusions, as the consequence doesn't work or change the behaviour of the child. This can be the case and is unfortunate. However, exclusion sends a clear message to pupils and parents that some behaviours are not acceptable. A fixed-term exclusion for me is a powerful tool to use. If you have repeat offenders, you need to then start demonstrating your graduated response to identify what else, alongside the exclusion, you are doing to change behaviour and support the child. Never shy away from suggesting a fixed-term exclusion for poor behaviour. The only caveat to this is to make sure that the exclusion isn't putting the child at further risk from a safeguarding perspective. Use of the government guidance on exclusions is always recommended.

Thinking point three

One of the Principals I worked with in the past used to have a set of what they called 'no-no behaviours'. They were explained to all children in assemblies at the start of the year and re-visited during the year. Our value words were the drivers to ensure these behaviours were discouraged. One of the 'no-no behaviours' was swearing at staff and we issued a fixed-term exclusion for these.

- What would your no-no behaviours be?
- How would you introduce these?
- How would you ensure they were consistently met?
- How would your behaviour system pick these up?
- Would you ALWAYS stick to the agreed sanction?

Jot down your thoughts.

Measuring the impact of the system

There are lots of other interventions, ideas and programmes that you can develop to support children who have challenging behaviour. We know as we discussed in the previous chapter that the SEND team can support, and you should look at this avenue first. Then you need to think about the SEMH side of things. How can you develop a set of systems that supports the needs of these children? We looked earlier at what provisions you could put in place (REACH, Bridge, dramatherapy), but you can also be creative and use other methods. Here are a few examples of to the systems I have used to support and re-engage pupils where detentions and exclusions have been racking up.

Pastoral Support Plan (PSP)

A PSP is used to identify key areas where a pupil is struggling and then to set SMART targets with them and their parents. Parental involvement is crucial – to be on a PSP, you will have tried lots of other supportive interventions and there will not have been much change. Parents and the child need to know how intense this method is. You need to set and review the targets each week and ensure the parents attend every meeting. Once you have agreed on the targets, they are sent to all staff and a small report card can be designed that can just be tick boxes against the targets. Make sure that you agree on suitable and achievable rewards for the pupil; they need to feel an accomplishment and you must keep motivation levels high. You also need to agree on sanctions for failing to meet the targets and parents need a daily phone call. It is really important that you persevere with this for at least a half term; it takes time to change engrained behaviour. A PSP is very time consuming and intense, but when done properly it really works and forges positive relationships between the school and parents who previously would not have engaged.

J-List

This was something I created while working in my first assistant head teacher role in Sheffield. We didn't have too many big hitters causing problems with behaviour. The school was outstanding and many of the children were focused, hardworking and came from very supportive backgrounds. As in all settings, though, there were some pupils who wouldn't engage and would consistently misbehave and cause issues around school. They become part of my J-List, a small group of pupils who had three targets to meet in every lesson and around school. Every member of staff was aware of them and they carried a pink report card to each lesson. The idea was to let them know that everyone was watching them and scrutinising their every move. Each week the head teacher and I would meet them as individuals and as a group to reflect on their week. We then reviewed targets, reviewed their successes and failures, and met with each pupil's parents. The idea was to build up successes, and then they could come off the pink report. Each week I would spend five minutes in staff briefings going through their targets and expectations. It was time consuming but enabled us to work closely with the pupils and their parents and to have a consistent school approach to tackling their behaviour.

SWAPP (Schools Wanting Alternative Placement Panel)

The idea with SWAPP is that it is a strategy for school-to-school support. Each month the key pastoral leaders meet up and discuss any pupils who may be causing concerns in their school. We present a few details about the child and what interventions have already been tried and then discuss if a SWAPP at another school for a period of time would help. The idea is that it may break a cycle for a child and give them a fresh start. It may show them the grass isn't greener and it also gives everyone some respite from challenging situations. It could also be used as part of an agreed 'managed move' process to avoid things like permanent exclusions.

Does it work? For some pupils, yes, and they stay at the receiving school for good. For others you end up passing the problem on, but for some pupils they come back to their host school and change their behaviour. For systems like this to work there needs to be honesty, trust and openness between the schools, and you have to use it as an early intervention to support change in behaviour, not as a last resort. You also need someone to chair the process and be independent of it all. We appointed two senior vice principals in Barnsley to chair the process. My colleague and I acted independently, so any pupils coming from our school were presented by another staff member from our school. We placed the SWAPP children into three categories: short, sharp shock (a short time, one to two weeks at another school to do as it says); respite (to give the pupil, the parents and the current school a period of respite from poor behaviour or poor relationships with other pupils); or a 'managed move' where the pupil would stay for at least a half term and eventually go on roll at the school. We made sure we built in regular reviews with both schools involved and the parents and pupil. No pupil was ever SWAPP'd unless the parents had approved and signed a referral form. We also built into the protocol that the head teacher of the receiving school had the right to cancel any SWAPP at any time. We also combined it to fit alongside the Fair Access Protocol that was used in Barnsley, creating clarity about the processes that schools would undertake before a child went to Fair Access.

What follows is a copy of the protocols we used, in case you ever want to try something like this.

SWAPP protocol

Aims and purpose

- To be an integral part of *early intervention* for vulnerable pupils and to be part of the 'blue' section of Fair Access, with an Assess, Plan, Do, Review approach

- To manage the mobility aspect of admissions and school transfers more efficiently and effectively

- To improve the quality of information that accompanies a pupil to his/her host school

- To improve pupil behaviour and attitudes via a completed managed move, a short, sharp shock or a part-time transfer to allow pupils to appreciate that all schools expect the same

- To give vulnerable and disadvantaged pupils a chance to succeed in another setting
- To promote, develop and encourage sharing of good practice by pastoral staff to benefit all pupils in Barnsley schools

Quality assurance

Schools who agree to take part in the SWAPP process will follow the 'practice' outlined next. To ensure there is clarity, fairness and rigour applied to the process, there will be:

- Two senior leaders nominated by the schools to:
    - review referrals prior to the meeting ensuring all criteria is met
    - chair the meeting and report to secondary head teachers once per term on the success of SWAPP

Practice

- Schools to identify pupils who would benefit from a fresh start, a short, sharp shock or a managed move
- SEN, Looked After Children and children on a child protection plan should be discussed at the nearest review meeting prior to referring them to SWAPP. Pupils who fall into these categories will only be allowed a SWAPP if there is evidence that all professionals agree in the latest minutes of the aforementioned meeting
- The two chairs will review the referrals to SWAPP prior to the meeting, ensuring that they meet the agreed protocol; if not they will be rejected
- Every SWAPP must take an Assess, Plan, Do, Review approach and use the 'Pastoral Support Plan' document that incorporates a review at week four. This is organised by the host school to determine the next steps
- Identification of pupils by degrees of disaffection BUT within the 'blue' area of the Fair Access flow chart. This includes, but is not exhaustive of:
    - Non-attendance
    - Persistent bullying (victim or perpetrator)
    - Persistent *low-level* disruption
    - Single serious incident
    - No more than **five** fixed-term exclusions (instances, NOT days)
- Schools can refer a maximum of two pupils per meeting and will 'receive' no more than two in any meeting

- Every SWAPP meeting will review previous SWAPPs and the month prior in order to assess whether there has been a positive change in behaviour if they have returned to their original school (this shows a positive impact of SWAPP)

- On a termly basis the SWAPP meeting will incorporate 'Behaviour and Attendance' priorities from the Local Authority. At this meeting schools will share good practice around key aspects to cascade into other settings

- The professional opinion of staff in individual schools must be trusted and the reasons for the SWAPP transparent

- Head teachers have the right to cancel a SWAPP at any point. Other than for this reason a SWAPP should run to at least the four-week review but not beyond a half term UNLESS agreed as part of the 'Pastoral Support Plan' during the Assess, Plan, Do, Review process

- All safeguarding concerns should be made clear and shared between safeguard leads of the schools involved

- Parents/carers must be involved throughout, and they must sign the SWAPP referral form and be involved in ALL reviews

- The SWAPP referral form must be completed fully and will be scrutinised at the pre-SWAPP meeting by the chairs

- The SWAPP panel must consist of one member from each school, even if there are no pupils from their school being referred at that meeting. A locality approach will be suggested to support the SWAPP

- Pupils will be registered as 'B' by the referring school and a guest by the host school. Communication should take place between both schools to ensure accuracy and for safeguarding purposes

- If a fixed-term exclusion is required as part of the SWAPP, the host school must firstly communicate with the referring school as the exclusion, and resulting paperwork will be completed and counted for the referring school

- Consideration for SWAPP will be given to pupils in Years 7-10. Year 11 pupils will not be considered, nor will the permanent managed move of a Year 10 pupil after Easter

- It is suggested as good practice and as part of the 'Pastoral Support Plan' that parents should sign up to and confirm that they agree to follow the policies of the host school

- A uniform will be provided by the host school for the duration of the SWAPP

This gives a flavour of some of the interventions and processes that I have used in my settings and as part of borough-wide approaches.

Rewards

There needs to be some form of a reward system in schools. Yes, in an ideal world it would be lovely that all children are internally motivated to work hard and succeed, and that success in their exams is their motivating factor. In the real world and in some disadvantaged areas, this just isn't the case.

A good starting point is to talk to the children. If you want them to be motivated and want them to achieve, ask them how they want to be rewarded: what would they like?

Hopefully you have a pupil leadership group set up. Use their voice and influence to find out what the children want and then set it up. Make sure you tailor your reward systems around the right age groups: what motivates a Year 7 pupil probably won't motivate a Year 11 pupil. There are also lots of companies out there who will have programmes and software to help you with this.

Here is a quick list of rewards and types of rewards I have used (these are in bold) or heard of:

- **Postcards**
- Points systems: 100 points = a certain prize
- **Prom and prom points**
- **End of year awards evenings**
- Form competitions
- **Bacon butty mornings**
- **Queue jump passes**
- Ice cream vans
- Parties
- **Cinema events**
- **Graduation ceremonies**
- **House systems**
- **Hot chocolate Friday**
- **Special mentions**

I am going to focus on two of these rewards in more detail. Before I do this, though, I want you to reflect on what we discussed in Chapter 1.

- What are your ethos and values? (If you are about positivity and celebration, then a reward system will come easy to you.)

- What happens if your setting's ethos is more academic and clinical?

■ How do you tailor a reward system around that?

The ethos of a school will most certainly influence the type of reward system that you can put in place. You must also ensure you delegate some of these responsibilities to your team. You may have another colleague who has responsibility for rewards. That is great, but you must ensure their ideas and systems strategically match what you are trying to achieve. You don't want conflicting systems. Every school has pastoral leaders, and you must delegate responsibility to them.

■ They need to take ownership of their year group: what will their rewards look like?

■ How do they match what you are trying to achieve?

Use your pastoral development plan to help you here. Plan to strategically incorporate rewards and then make your pastoral leaders your enablers.

Refer back to my development plan. It had some key targets for rewards in the personal development strand. Section 3.3 stated, 'celebrate the achievements of the consistently good students in a number of ways'. This was then allocated to certain colleagues, where they would evidence their work to meet this and therefore develop different ways to celebrate achievements. This type of planning allows everyone to work as individuals but also under the same strategic heading. That is why your development plan is so crucial.

To support a new reward system and approach to behaviour management, sometimes you have to start again and launch something new. This is a risk, and you have to be brave and consistent with this. If you stay in a role long enough in one school, you will have to keep adapting and tweaking things.

> **Empowering the positive anecdote: thoughts for the 'scenario'**
>
> I was not happy with what we were doing, though. We needed to move with the times. Children were ready to learn but we weren't pushing them enough, and our approach didn't promote celebration or success. It was more like control. The head teacher and I met and agreed to revamp the system and the approach. I spent a few months researching other schools, asking colleagues and working with a group of staff and pupils in school to look at what to do. We came up with the notion of 'empowering the positive'. Too often we weren't positive enough: our system, our teaching, our rewards didn't promote or establish enough positivity. If we reflect back to earlier chapters, I am a big believer in experiences driving feelings, and feelings driving behaviour, so we had to ensure our children's experiences were positive. We re-wrote the behaviour system, introduced systems that promoted positive approaches and celebrated success at every chance we could. The house system was an integral part of this, and I will come to that shortly. The impact was happier children, more productive children and less situations of conflict. It didn't always work that well and we had to redefine a few things, but with considerable drive, lots of assemblies and lots of celebrations, we achieved what we set out to do: a new system that was embraced by all.

> Did it improve the behaviour? For some, no, but it did improve the feel of the school; it was almost tangible. Part of the work for empowering the positive was a teacher booklet and a teacher toolkit that I wrote and made for everyone.

Types of rewards

House system

The house system is nothing new. The resurgence of these is probably down to the magical wizard Harry Potter and his adventures. Most schools now have a house system; however, I know a lot of house systems really don't run as they should and don't have the desired impact. Why is this? Two reasons: (1) there needs to be someone driving the system and having responsibility for it, and (2) they don't engage all stakeholders.

Logo

You have to have a logo for each house, and it needs a design and a colour. Think about how you want to choose these. They could be linked to the school or famous people, planets, whatever you think, but ask the children!

Figure 4.3 shows a design from one of my settings.

Motto

Make sure you have a motto or a set of values for each of your houses. You need to ensure that each house has one or two of the Academy value words too. This helps you with promoting these, and you can base assemblies and PSHE around these.

Figure 4.3

Charities

Make sure you have a charity tied to each house, and then every term you can have charity events and raise money for your requested charity. These can be any charities, but to create a true community school, you should try and choose local charities that work within the community.

House captains

This system is perfect for developing leadership. Appoint house captains and vice captains. You can have a house council or house ambassadors. Use these leaders to help drive your ideas and to create a link to the rest of the children in the house. They come up with brilliant ideas and this creates such a good buy-in.

Competitions

This goes without saying. Involve staff in competitions and have separate score charts for them – it brings out the best in all stakeholders. Don't forget parents and governors too. To ensure that all stakeholders are involved, think about how you want to organise these events. You could have a big House Week event each half term where you and the person leading the house organise lots of wacky events. You should also think about how to include departments in this. In both my recent settings, we have had weekly competitions which are organised and run by departments. A few examples come next (Figures 4.4–4.6).

History example

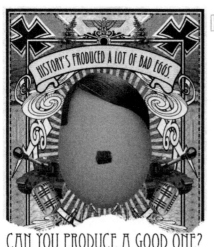

Figure 4.4

Example result sheets and register

House Week Competition Results Sheet

Event		Skill	
Faculty		Date	

	Points	House	Student Name	Staff Name
1st				
2nd				
3rd				
4th				
5th				

Please hand completed results and register sheets to ……

Figure 4.5

House rewards/celebrations

Whatever happens, you must share the successes with all stakeholders. If you think strategically, you can tie in various aspects of school life and improvement to the house competition. You can track house attendance, house engagement in learning, house progress, house attainment and have individual totals and prizes for these. We had big banners that we hung down from the building on House Celebration weeks. Make sure you celebrate success and effort as much as you can.

You can build in termly house rewards such as cinema events, roller discos and whatever the children come up with. Work closely with your PE department and base Sports Day around the houses. You can have opening ceremonies, banners, songs, face painting and so much more. You must then finish the year off with a house champion and a whole school celebration event.

- Can you get all pupils into a space in the school and celebrate all of this together?
- Can you have trophies, banners, confetti, videos?
- Can you have a staff champion?

We had various staff competitions through the year and we even had a staff wooden spoon competition. Give trophies for the most house points for children in each house, for the most progress and for the most money raised, and give the house captains a prize. Celebrate, celebrate and celebrate! The bigger you make it, the more the children will love it and the more buy-in you have. A house system, when done well, really does help to promote a positive culture.

House Week Competition Register

Event		Skill	
Faculty		Date	

Barts

Name & Form	Score
1.	
2.	
3.	
4.	
5.	
6.	
7.	
8.	
9.	
10.	
11.	
12.	
13.	
14.	
15.	
16.	
17.	
18.	
19.	
20.	

Bede

Name & Form	Score
1.	
2.	
3.	
4.	
5.	
6.	
7.	
8.	
9.	
10.	
11.	
12.	
13.	
14.	
15.	
16.	
17.	
18.	
19.	
20.	

Rolleston

Name & Form	Score
1.	
2.	
3.	
4.	
5.	
6.	
7.	
8.	
9.	
10.	
11.	
12.	
13.	
14.	
15.	
16.	
17.	
18.	
19.	
20.	

York

Name & Form	Score
1.	
2.	
3.	
4.	
5.	
6.	
7.	
8.	
9.	
10.	
11.	
12.	
13.	
14.	
15.	
16.	
17.	
18.	
19.	
20.	

Figure 4.6

Key Stage 3 Graduation

The second reward system I thought I would share with you was one I developed myself in Sheffield. Pupils in the school were producing excellent work and there was a real drive around excellence, but the reward system we had in place wasn't great. It was outdated and the children didn't see any value in it. I had just been appointed assistant head teacher for inclusion and wanted to re-vamp the reward system. I firstly met with some pupils to ask about what they wanted. It was about gratification for the effort they were putting in as well as the work they produced. They also wanted recognition for their efforts both inside and outside the school via extra-curricular teams, charity work and so on. Strategically I met with the rest of the senior team to look at this and I wanted to combine what the children said with our values and drivers at that time. I then brought in some heads of department to get their viewpoint form a teaching and learning perspective. What I came up with was the Key Stage 3 Graduation. I used the design skills of the head of the art, design and technology department who helped me create the systems that follow.

The school was looking to develop the following values within all our stakeholders:

- To be *skilled independent learners*
- To be *leaders*
- To be *active global citizens*
- To have a *positive contribution* in our community

I based all the rewards around these four headings, and pupils could gain rewards under each heading in every department and from their pastoral team, too. We even created a SLT one. There are two examples shown in Figures 4.7–4.14.

English Key Stage 3 Graduation rewards

Figure 4.7

Figure 4.8

Figure 4.9

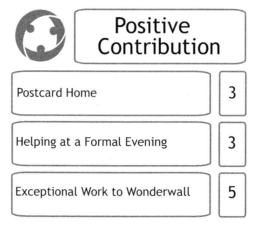

Figure 4.10

As you can see, there was a logo for each value as well and, depending upon the department, you could win more rewards in some areas than others. I made sure that all generic rewards like postcards were given equal weighting and all departments had to agree with each other's scoring so that it was fair. There were obvious differences in some areas such as physical education, but as everyone was involved, it was fair and we had a consistent school-wide reward system.

Physical education Key Stage 3 Graduation rewards

Figure 4.11

Figure 4.12

The idea was that children in Years 7-9 could earn all these rewards in each lesson and, using the school's virtual learning environment, they had a platform where they could log their reward, what it was for and which teacher approved it. I simply asked staff to then check that they were happy with the awards and they were

Figure 4.13

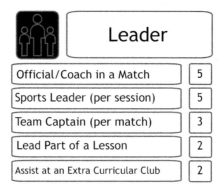

Figure 4.14

logged on the child's record on SIMS. It was easy, then, for the children to have a record of which 'value' they were more competent in and which subject areas. These rewards formed one part of their graduation. At the end of Year 9, we held a graduation ceremony where every pupil was awarded a scroll.

They graduated in the following areas:

Academic effort – pupils were given an effort score in their lessons, and this was averaged out across every subject and each of the three years.

Academic progress – before progress 8 arrived, we did something similar where we mapped out their progress from their Key Stage 2 scores in English and maths (this was the data we had in 2009) to what they should achieve at the end of Key Stage 3.

Community contribution – this was the total amount of reward points given over the three years from what they had logged based on the department sheets mentioned earlier. We then subtracted any negative behaviour points they got to get a total and rank the year group.

Attendance and punctuality – the last strand took into account their attendance and punctuality over the three years.

Pupils could graduate in each area with a **Distinction**, a **Merit**, a **Pass** or **With Concerns**.

We then averaged these out to give an overall graduation level. Pupils were awarded a scroll and we then used all this data to help us in Key Stage 4. Attendance and punctuality data were used with our education welfare officers. We used the academic progress to determine their curriculum and option choices, and it allowed us to highlight pupils who might need more vocational choices. We then used the effort and contribution data to see who was buying into school life and who could be our prefects or ambassadors of the future. We used some of the *with concerns* data to highlight pupils going into Year 10 who might need to be monitored from a pastoral perspective. It really was an effective whole school system, and the children and staff bought into it, as did the parents. We started to use it with transition, too. Pupils were aware of what was coming, and how they could succeed and be rewarded.

Figure 4.15 shows the landing page for the pupils. They had to click on a logo in a subject to bring up the list of rewards behind it and then fill in a data form that sat behind it. I must say that Jenny Meadows and Alan Wenham, who were the data gurus behind this, were simply awesome and without them it wouldn't have functioned!

I hope this chapter has given you an insight into the importance of systems and that while everyone will have an opinion on behaviour and rewards, you must reflect on what is right for you and your setting. You have to be brave as a leader of inclusion and go with what you think is right, and if you do your research, involve key players and review what you do. You won't go too far wrong. Remember that everyone has behaviour to deal with, and everyone will think they can do it better than you. Listen, respond, but stick to your principles, too. The systems are the key!

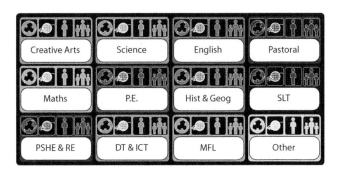

Figure 4.15 Key Stage 3 graduation landing page

This quote always sticks with me about this. You have to listen and you have to reflect, but then you shape things in the way you think are best. You lead!

> A genuine leader is not a searcher for consensus, but a moulder of consensus.
>
> (Martin Luther King Jr)

Leading inclusion scenario four

You are appointed assistant head teacher in charge of pastoral care at a new school. You have previously been in charge of Key Stage 4 in another school and been responsible for excellent outcomes and forward-thinking work. Your new school has been placed in special measures and has been academised as part of that process. The trust that has taken over the school is relatively small with three other secondary schools. Your head teacher and CEO want a new system to be developed for monitoring both behaviour and rewards. The CEO wants to use a trust model that is used in the other three schools. They are all outstanding but serve a vastly different catchment to yours. Your new school serves a diverse and highly disadvantaged area where ambition and aspirations are low. You want to develop a system that promotes success and positivity, but your CEO wants the school to have tight systems around controlling behaviour.

- How do you tackle this situation?
- How do you get your own way?
- Can you?
- How would you start to plan this piece of work so that it appeases your head teacher and CEO, but utilises your experience and values?

Chapter 4 references and research

Cotton, D. (2010). *The Effect of Structural Listening and Learning Has on Pupils and Schools Following Incidents Involving Physical Intervention.* www.pbstraining.co.uk

Cotton, D. (2013). *A Design Research Study in One School Piloting an Information Technology (IT) Based Application (App).* Unpublished.

Department for Education. (2017). *Exclusion from Maintained Schools, Academies and Pupil Referral Units. Statutory Guidance for Those with Legal Responsibilities in Relation to Exclusion.* DFE-00184-2017.

Dreikurs, R., and Grey, L. (1993). *The New Approach to Discipline, Logical Consequences.* Plume.

Smith, B. A. (2005). *Saturday Detention as an Effective Disciplinary Consequence: High School Administrators' Perspective* (1st January 2005). Dissertations Collection for University of Connecticut. Paper AAI3180258.

5 Safeguarding

If there is one part of my role that has changed the most in the time I have been doing it, it is safeguarding. The responsibilities, processes, systems and knowledge required to do the role have increased exponentially. Gone are the days where you had a single designated safeguarding lead or child protection lead teacher.

Safeguarding is not and cannot be one person's responsibility. Everyone needs to be mindful of it and you need a safeguarding team to help you complete your role effectively.

This chapter is going to focus on possibly the most important part of the role of a leader of inclusion. Over the next pages I will look at what safeguarding actually is in a secondary school. The chapter will cover some of the statutory requirements that you will need to have in place. It will also look at the different methods and processes you can use to train your staff and to ensure you have clear, strategic oversight of safeguarding in your setting. There will be thinking opportunities for you and the chance to understand what must be done in certain situations, giving you the knowledge of how to do things in a robust and accurate way. The scenario at the end of the chapter is a challenging one that I hope no one would have to face, but you and your staff have to be skilled to deal with whatever happens. Use the information in the chapter and research some of the guidance to help you answer the scenario.

Safeguarding and child protection

Firstly, let's start with what each of these are.

Safeguarding is the actions that are taken to promote the welfare of children and protect them from harm. This relates to all the things we can do on a day-to-day basis to protect children from harm.

Some examples of these actions are:

- A caring ethos

- A safe and secure site

- Disclosure and Barring Service (DBS)-checked staff

- Working together and sharing information with external agencies

- Children knowing they have adults who care about them and that they can trust

- Skilled, knowledgeable and vigilant staff

- A simple and well-known reporting system

- Clear policies and rules

Child protection is related to the systems and processes that are used to protect children who have been or who are likely to suffer harm. This includes a formal plan with safety statements and clear targets that are reviewed regularly.

All teachers need to regularly read and understand their school's child protection and safeguarding policy. You have a duty of care to ensure you contribute to the safety of children. Make sure you know this document inside out and pay particular attention to what you must do if you have a concern around the child. This document should also give you detailed information about what the signs of abuse may look like. As the leader of safeguarding, it will be your responsibility to keep this document up-to-date and in line with government regulations.

The aim of this chapter is to support you with the leadership of safeguarding. It is not a one-person job. You need to build a team around you that is skilled at recognising any signs of abuse and that has a responsibility to act on these signs. This is where your pastoral team and the job description that you write for them are crucial. Make sure you train up each one of them to a designated safeguarding lead level and assign them all as deputy designated safeguarding leads. Your pastoral staff will begin to see the signs and start to recognise when children may be at risk.

As a senior leader of inclusion, you do not have the capacity to be involved in all the operational aspects of safeguarding and child protection. You have to have strategic oversight of the responsibility that lies with a designated safeguarding lead, but you must delegate some responsibilities to your team. All the colleagues that I have worked with have stepped up to the plate and enjoyed this extra responsibility; it also gave me the confidence and reassurance that all of our children were safe.

Everyone's business and it can happen here

A key leadership strategy for safeguarding is to develop a culture where your children's safety is paramount. You need to instil confidence and a belief in your staff about how to safeguard children and what to look out for. Staff need up-to-date and relevant CPD along with clear whistleblowing policies and procedures that are trusted and understood.

There is a myth in the teaching profession that only certain people are privy to safeguarding and child protection information, and that it should be a guarded secret. Yes, there are aspects of child protection that must remain confidential. However, in order to run a school where the children's best interests are at the forefront of all we do, our staff must be aware of the difficulties our children face and what may be going on in their lives outside of school. It is important that you regularly update your staff with the right information about the children they will teach. This can be short, sharp and to the point. You don't need to disclose anything confidential, but you do need to make them aware that the children's behaviour or attitude may be different when they teach them. It is not right or fair to set vulnerable children up to fail by not sharing information with colleagues who can then plan to support their needs in the classroom. Vulnerable children need to develop positive relationships in school and to build trust with the adults that they see on a daily basis. This requires a caring and watchful community.

Thinking point one

- How would you develop an open, trusting environment within your setting?

- What could you do as a leader of inclusion to promote, model and quality assure this?

- What methods of communication and training could you utilise to embed this?

Jot down your ideas.

Operational safeguarding

Part of developing your staff's understanding of child protection and safeguarding is to make sure that everyone is aware of the law and the statutory responsibilities that working in a school comes with. At the same time you must break down the jargon that goes with this. It is really important that you interweave the systems that you use to support children on a daily basis. Again, you can highlight the importance of the graduated response; the importance of interventions and support for a child; the importance of special educational needs support; and finally how crucial a timely and accurate referral must be if any staff have a safeguarding concern.

Recording

It is imperative that you instil a culture within the school to report any type of concern a member of the staff has. There are no silly questions, and if there is enough of a concern for someone to think about it, then they need to log it. You must also ensure that all of your wider safeguarding team logs everything and logs all of their actions too.

Electronic systems are widely in use. These vary from CPOMS, to safeguard software, to classcharts. They're all excellent, and I would suggest you research them all and find the software that is best for your setting and for your children. Log everything, action everything and attach all the relevant paperwork, interventions, reports and other relevant documents onto the system. All the information should be in one place so you can safeguard the child and have the information at your fingertips for when you may need it.

Reporting and managing a disclosure

Once you have received your initial concern, the designated safeguarding lead should investigate it fully. It is not the responsibility of teaching staff or associate staff to do this, and they will not have the appropriate training. By investigating it fully, you and your colleagues will then decide what the appropriate next steps are to safeguard this child.

Our job is to find out the facts about the disclosure and get as many factual details down as possible. You will have to think about how you support the pupil or member of staff after the disclosure. There is a chance that they will be deeply upset by what has happened, and will need to be reassured and supported afterwards. Once you have all the details, you then need decide what action to take. Making reference to the threshold document for your Local Authority and getting advice from a duty social worker can be helpful. This gives you the chance to explain the disclosure and what you have investigated, and it allows you to ask for what they think the next steps are. This could be a full referral, or it could be for you as the designated safeguarding lead (DSL) to action by calling parents, speaking with other agencies or starting an Early Help Assessment. For every referral or conversation with social care, you must log who you spoke to and what the advice and outcome was.

Don't forget you can delegate some of these investigations to your team. If you don't expose them to the situations, they won't learn and they won't develop the confidence to deal with difficult situations. As you train and skill up your team, they may come to you with regular updates and also seek your advice about what the next steps are. This is where up-to-date information that is stored all in one place will help you to unreservedly make these decisions. An accurate timeline of events stored on your electronic software gives you an indication of previous concerns, patterns of behaviour or details of any external agency involvement.

Thresholds

Every Local Authority will have a multi-agency threshold document that you will have to refer to in order to decide whether or not to make a referral to children's social services. This will have been developed by the local safeguarding partnership, and it should be a document that you and your team know inside out. It will describe the four-tiered levels of support, and you must then cross reference all of your concerns and your timeline of evidence against these tiers to determine your next steps.

The four-tiered thresholds

Tier 1

Requiring universal services – children with no additional need.

The majority of families within your setting will fall into this tier and will have their needs met at home, at school and in their lives on a daily basis.

Tier 2

Requiring early intervention – children with some additional needs.

Children in this tier have a low-level additional need that can usually be met with short-term interventions. They may require multi-agency intervention to prevent their needs escalating or to prevent their circumstances from deteriorating.

Tier 3

Requiring targeted and enhanced support – children with additional, complex needs.

These are children with high level, unmet needs and those with complex needs that will require longer term intervention from services. Children in this tier need careful assessment and analysis to ensure that their needs are met and prevent further escalation of risk. They may be eligible for work from children's social services.

Tier 4

Requiring acute/statutory intervention – children with complex and/or acute needs.

These are children with needs that are acute, either in terms of urgency, complexity or the degree of risk they are exposed to. Children in this tier require emergency or urgent protection, child protection or care proceedings. Children with complex needs requiring nursing or inpatient care, including those with mental health problems, all have T4 needs.

The continuum of needs

This can be referred to as the 'windscreen' and is used in lots of authorities. Figure 5.1 is an example of how Local Authorities use the tiers to produce a continuum of

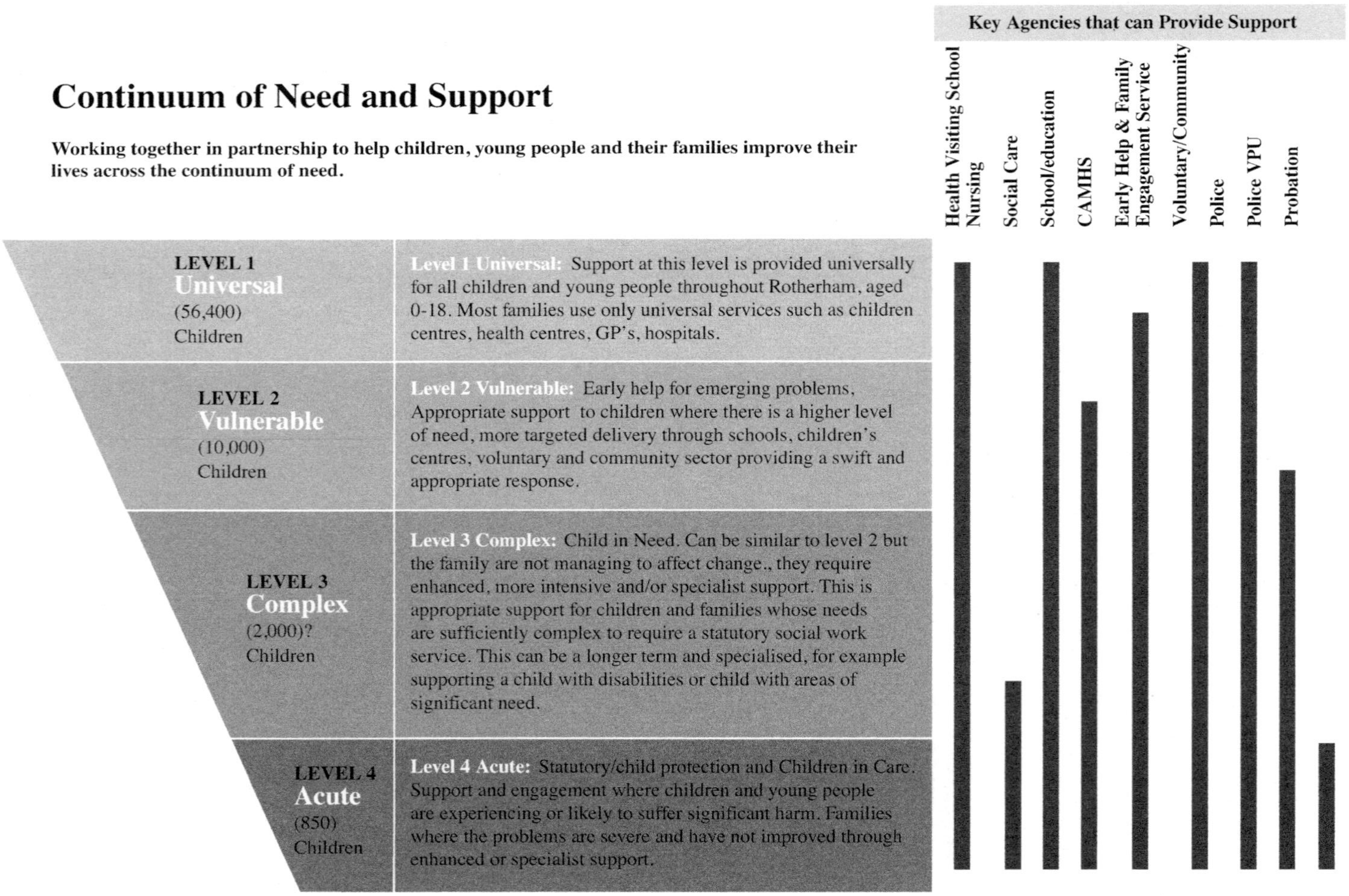

80 Safeguarding

Continuum of Need and Support

Working together in partnership to help children, young people and their families improve their lives across the continuum of need.

Key Agencies that can Provide Support
Health Visiting School Nursing
Social Care
School/education
CAMHS
Early Help & Family Engagement Service
Voluntary/Community
Police
Police VPU
Probation

LEVEL 1 Universal (56,400) Children — **Level 1 Universal:** Support at this level is provided universally for all children and young people throughout Rotherham, aged 0-18. Most families use only universal services such as children centres, health centres, GP's, hospitals.

LEVEL 2 Vulnerable (10,000) Children — **Level 2 Vulnerable:** Early help for emerging problems. Appropriate support to children where there is a higher level of need, more targeted delivery through schools, children's centres, voluntary and community sector providing a swift and appropriate response.

LEVEL 3 Complex (2,000)? Children — **Level 3 Complex:** Child in Need. Can be similar to Level 2 but the family are not managing to affect change., they require enhanced, more intensive and/or specialist support. This is appropriate support for children and families whose needs are sufficiently complex to require a statutory social work service. This can be a longer term and specialised, for example supporting a child with disabilities or child with areas of significant need.

LEVEL 4 Acute (850) Children — **Level 4 Acute:** Statutory/child protection and Children in Care. Support and engagement where children and young people are experiencing or likely to suffer significant harm. Families where the problems are severe and have not improved through enhanced or specialist support.

Figure 5.1 (from Rotherham Children's Safeguarding Board: https://rotherhamscb.proceduresonline.com/pdfs/multiagency_threshold_descriptors.pdf)

needs. Whatever Local Authority you are part of will have one of these. Make sure that you use it and reference it when making referrals.

My Local Authority is Rotherham, and it uses a slightly different one, but it is still on the same premise. Each one of these 'tiers' will have detailed descriptors that go with it to help you with your decision-making process.

When you have a concern and you think you need to make a referral to social services, cross reference your evidence to each tier before you make the call. If your evidence fits within Tiers 1 and 2, it is likely that you can solve the issue within school or that an Early Help Assessment can be done to support the child and family.

Call social services if you are in doubt and present them the information you have and ask for advice. Every authority that I have worked in has a triage desk where you can ask these questions and get advice. Remember, you must be factual, take the name of the person that you speak to, any actions that they suggest and add the date for the safeguarding timeline.

As the designated safeguarding lead and the school professional, you may know this child best. You may also know the family best and the situation they are faced with. If you feel that the advice you are given is incorrect and you disagree, then you must escalate this. Every safeguarding partnership will have an escalation process and if you have any doubts as a professional, you need to act on them. It is about having a professional dialogue around the safety of the child. Don't feel embarrassed, don't be nervous; give your evidence and your feelings in a concise and accurate way and hopefully you'll get the best result for the child.

Responses

If you feel there is enough evidence against the thresholds, you will need to write a full referral adding any evidence you have against the criteria and you will need to send this to social services for them to complete an assessment. As designated safeguarding lead it is your responsibility to chase up the outcome of the assessment. The allocated social worker, or the person you initially spoke to, may not have the capacity to return your call and inform you of the outcome.

The outcomes will be one of the following, which will form part of the assessment process, as indicated in the Children's Act 1989.

1 **No action taken** – social care will assess that you can meet the needs of the child and the family, and that you can call the parent or carer, or arrange a meeting with them, to manage the risk and offer support.

2 **Early Help Assessment and team around the family support** – this is where you or one of your colleagues will become the lead professional in supporting the family. You will meet with the family and complete a detailed document that highlights any concerns about the needs of the children. This is the primary source of intervention that you will come across in your role as designated

safeguarding lead. I would advise you to delegate the lead professional role to your wider safeguarding team in some of these cases. They will know the child and the family in more detail than you and they will also have the time and capacity to lead and action support that comes from the regular team around the family meetings. As designated safeguarding lead, you must have oversight of all of these, and you must make sure that the actions taken are timely and effective. A regular meeting with your safeguarding team is vital to keep you up to date.

3 **Child in need (Section 17)** – a child is considered 'in need' if:

- They are unlikely to achieve or maintain, or to have the opportunity to achieve or maintain, a reasonable standard of health or development without provision of services from the Local Authority.

- Their health or development is likely to be significantly impaired, or further impaired, without the provision of services from the Local Authority.

- They have a disability (including blindness, deafness or dumbness), mental disorders and permanent illnesses, injuries or congenital deformities.

Children in need may be:

- Children with SEND

- Young carers

- Children who have committed a crime

- Children whose parents are in prison

- Asylum-seeking children

    If a Section 17 assessment and outcome is agreed to, the Local Authority will set up a child in need plan which will indicate the level of support being given to the child and/or family. It will be reviewed regularly, within three months at first and at least every six months thereafter. As designated safeguarding lead, or a delegated member of your safeguarding team, you'll be responsible for completing any work identified. You must produce reports for the review meetings and the school must be represented. Your setting will dictate how many Early Help Assessments, child in need or child protection children you have. As designated safeguarding lead you must lead on some of these, but not all.

4 **Section 47 assessment** – if professionals feel that the child is at risk of serious harm, then a strategy meeting is called. A social worker will lead the meeting and, as designated safeguarding lead, you'll be expected to attend. Make sure you prepare for these. This is where your log timeline and evidence base really help you to evidence vulnerability. Take as much evidence as you can that is

relevant to the meeting; it is vital that all information is shared. Remember, what you hear in these meetings is strictly confidential.

The strategy meeting will determine the next steps, and you need to be prepared that you will be asked for your opinion and what you think should happen based on the evidence that you have heard. A Section 47 assessment will come from the outcome of the strategy meeting. If a Section 47 assessment is agreed to, then the social worker will complete this and there will be an initial child protection conference called within 15 days. For this conference, as designated safeguarding lead, you'll be asked to submit a detailed report on an agreed proforma to the Local Authority and also to the parents. Make sure the content is factual, detailed and meets the requirements set out by the local safeguarding partnership. A child can be placed on a child protection plan for one of the following categories:

- Physical abuse
- Sexual abuse
- Emotional abuse
- Neglect

Child protection conferences

These are called as either initial conferences to determine a child protection plan for a child, or to review a previous plan, its actions and what the next steps will be. As designated safeguarding lead you should attend these but, again, you may delegate some of these to your safeguarding team. At the conference you will be asked to contribute about a child's education and any successes or areas of concern. These will have already been highlighted in the report you sent before the conference. At the end of the conference, you will be asked to scale the current situation, usually between 1 and 10, where 1 indicates the child is at significant risk. You will also be asked to confirm what category the plan should be classed under and whether the child should continue on the plan or not. The introduction of the new General Data Protection Regulations (GDPR) have caused quite a lot of concerns amongst staff regarding what they can and can't share. The point to remember here is **safeguarding and child protection top trumps it all**. You must not hold back from sharing anything about a concern relating to the safety of a child because of GDPR breaches. Their safety outweighs all of this.

Allegations against staff

As designated safeguarding lead there will come a time when you have to deal with an allegation against a member of the staff. We discussed earlier in the chapter about developing a culture of safeguarding, ensuring that all staff are vigilant and you sending the message that 'it can happen here', alongside promoting a child to speak up. An allegation doesn't have to be sexual to cause concern. It could be related to inappropriate behaviour, the use of bad language, threats or physical harm. It is important to note here that if you are working in a setting where physical restraint is used that there is a framework identified within the child protection policy and behaviour policy, and that staff are fully trained by a recognised body. It is also important to remind you that any allegations against the principal must be reported to the Chair of Governors, and any allegations against the Chair of Governors to the CEO or recognised leadership body.

Local Authority Designated Officer (LADO)

As DSL, you have a statutory duty to report any allegations to the LADO. The LADO's job is to manage all child protection allegations made against staff and volunteers who work with children. You will have the LADO's number and name in your child protection and safeguarding policy, and it can also be found on your local partnership's website.

If you are faced with an allegation, then the LADO will want all the factual information and all the details about the child and the adult involved. They will advise you on the steps that you must take. You should also be in regular contact with your HR lead or company about the allegations. They will also advise you and be involved in some way. If the allegation isn't related to the principal, then one of the first steps you must take is to inform the principal of the allegation.

A formal investigation may be launched, and as designated safeguarding lead you may be required to lead all or part of this and produce a written report. I have led several of these, and while they are never easy, they should be conducted in a professional and confidential manner alongside any HR/safeguarding policies and procedures your establishment adheres to. It can feel quite intimidating to lead these, and my advice is that you should talk to your principal and HR lead to ask for advice and also refer to the relevant policies. They will outline the process you need to take.

Thinking point two

You have a pupil who has just been placed on a child protection plan under the category of sexual abuse. The adults involved in the case are also under investigation from the police, so all the information about the plan and the situation is highly confidential. The pupil will need lots of emotional support and care.

- How do you get the message out to your colleagues about this situation without breaking any confidentiality?

- What methods could you use to inform them of the difficulties the child faces and how could they report any concerns back to you?

- Finally, and most importantly, how will you as the designated safeguarding lead support the child on a day-to-day basis?

Jot down your ideas about how you would do this.

Developing a culture – strategic safeguarding

As designated safeguarding lead, you set the tone and the culture for safeguarding in your setting, just like the principal sets the ethos and values of the school. As a DSL you should be modelling your work all the time. You should be visible; you should be supporting children; you should be challenging any inappropriate behaviour by staff and pupils; and your actions should model what you expect others to do.

This helps to create a vigilant culture and one that promotes professional respect. As a leader of this you should be communicating your culture at every opportunity you get. Deliver assemblies, write newsletters, use social media – communicate your message as often as you can, and each message should have some form of safeguarding intertwined in it.

One of the key aspects of promoting a safe culture is the subliminal messages that you send to perspective candidates. Make sure when embarking on a recruitment that you follow all the guidance about safer recruitment. Make sure your advert highlights references being taken, a full enhanced DBS check and also to offer face-to-face tours of the school. This can be invaluable to meet potential colleagues, but it also dissuades adults who may have a chequered past or who may be a risk to children. When you are shortlisting candidates, ensure that you ask for details about any gaps in employment and make sure dates of employment match up.

Make any offers of employment subject to two positive references and a full, enhanced DBS check, and ensure that on your panel there is at *least* one member of staff trained in safer recruitment *and* one governor trained. A well developed and thorough safeguarding culture will quickly become well known in your area, and this in itself can act as a deterrent to any adults who may pose a risk to children.

Single central record

The single central record (SCR) is a database of all your staff's pre-appointment checks and it must cover the following people:

- All staff, including trainee teachers on salaried routes, agency and third-party staff who work at the school.

The minimum information you should have is the following:

- An identity check – this can be a passport and driving license, and normally would also be a bill that shows the person's latest address
- A barred list check

- An enhanced DBS certificate/check
- Further checks on people who have lived or worked outside of the UK
- A prohibited from teaching check
- A check and copy of professional qualifications
- A check to establish, where required, the person's right to work in the UK

For academies and free schools, when recruiting for a leadership position, you must also include a Section 128 check. It is also good practice to run this check for your governors.

As designated safeguarding lead you may not necessarily be in charge of populating the SCR. This may be delegated to a business manager or someone who has oversight of recruitment. It is vital that you regularly meet to discuss the SCR and, as designated safeguarding lead, that you are happy that it contains all the relevant information. It is useful to add a tab at the bottom of the SCR where you can log and date when you have quality assured and checked the record throughout the year. One of the most important things for you to consider is that there must never be a gap of information on the SCR. If something doesn't apply to a member of staff, don't leave the box blank; put N/A inside of it. The SCR will usually be the first thing that an OFSTED inspector asks for on the first day of any inspection. As designated safeguarding lead you will be required to talk through the SCR and bring up various pieces of information the inspector requests. To be clear, if your SCR isn't accurate and has gaps, the inspector will change the nature of the inspection and it is likely the school would fall into special measures. There are lots of software programmes that can help you with this and not every SCR is the same; I would say design one that is best for you, your setting and your staff, but make sure it contains *all* of the required information.

Thinking point three

Reflect on your current setting. Make a list of the staff who you think should be on the SCR as they are likely to undertake regulated activity in your school. After you have done this, go and see your DSL, or whoever is responsible for the SCR, and ask them to see if you have missed anyone. Ask them if you can see what it looks like for CPD.

Make your list and then go and speak to your DSL.

Induction and training

Part of establishing your culture is to ensure that your staff members are fully trained and knowledgeable about child protection and safeguarding. It is up to you as designated safeguarding lead to keep abreast of the changes and to cascade your knowledge down to your staff. This can be done in various ways, but generally it's through a detailed induction and through regular professional development.

Induction

There will most likely be another senior leader in your school who will lead on some form of induction for new staff, and they may also lead on this for initial teacher training (ITT) students and other trainees. It is vital that child protection and safeguarding plays a big part of this induction. As designated safeguarding lead you will need to spend time with the new staff, introducing yourself, establishing your culture and explaining your systems and processes. I find that it is always useful to ask the induction lead to put on a 30-minute safeguarding session within the first day or two of new members of staff starting. This gives you the chance to reinforce the culture and it gives them the chance to familiarise themselves with the school, with what you expect and with you and your standards. It is also a really good opportunity to highlight any contextual safeguarding issues for your setting.

Professional development

As the senior leadership team starts to plan the training for the year ahead, make sure you link with them and ask for at least two or three whole staff sessions on child protection and safeguarding. All staff should have face-to-face safeguarding training every two years. These days it is more beneficial to do the official training online, but you must ensure you back that up with face-to-face sessions.

As well as the first day induction, it is always useful to highlight contextual safeguarding for your setting and any topical issues that are prevalent. It may be useful to subscribe to a safeguarding package, as it can provide detailed information that you can distribute to staff, and also provide scenarios and tasks that can help staff put this knowledge into practice. An excellent method that one of my old safeguarding leads devised was to send out a half termly quiz. Random staff were selected, including SLT and governors, and they were given several questions to test their knowledge. It was done in a friendly and non-intrusive manner whilst still promoting our safeguarding culture. At the end of the quiz there was a chance for the staff to highlight any areas that they needed further support with, and we then tailored this information to our next training session. An example of one of these quizzes is in Figure 5.2.

You must also remember that you must not leave your own knowledge underdeveloped. Make sure you go on regular safeguarding courses and regularly read up on safeguarding matters. You have to keep your governors fully up to speed and train them up, so they're aware of what to look for and what to ask when holding you to account.

Safeguarding staff survey January 2020

As part of our rigorous QA safeguarding schedule, every term we will randomly select members of staff to complete a quick survey about safeguarding. This will allow us to monitor effectiveness of our training and help ensure staff feel confident in safeguarding our children every day.
Please complete this form and return to Mark Allen – Trust Senior Vice Principal –

If you have any queries, please don't hesitate to see any of the designated safeguarding team.

Ring the correct letter or write the answer in the space provided.

Question 1: Which of these are forms of domestic abuse?

A	Controlling behaviour
B	Adolescent to parent violence and abuse
C	Verbal abuse
D	All of these

Question 2: What is fabricated illness?

A	A child constantly saying their ill to not attend school
B	A child has suffered or is likely to suffer significant harm through the deliberate acts of their parents bringing on illness or the impression of illness.
C	A child has been diagnosed with an illness by their parents

Question 3: What percentage of children in a secondary school are classed as a carer?

A	50%
B	10%
C	20%

Question 4: Who is the Looked After Children lead at our school? What is their role?

| Looked After Children Lead | |
| Their role is | |

Question 5: Which of these is true?

A	1 in 3 children who are sexually abused by an adult do not tell anyone
B	Non-contact activities such as watching or producing sexual images is not classed as abuse
C	Sexual abuse is perpetrated by adult males and adult females

Figure 5.2a

If you want to be sure that you have a safeguarding culture that is well-developed and vigilant, then you must spend time giving information out and leading regular training. Some colleagues won't always know what to look for, won't have any experience, and will also need regular updates. Remember to include your front of house staff in this training and make sure they are fully up to date on the signing in procedures, making sure you have different-coloured lanyards for different levels of supervision.

Question 6: What does LADO stand for:

A	Local Authority Designated Officer
B	Legal Adviser for Domestic Occurrences
C	Local Authority Delegated Office

Question 7: What is the role of the LADO?

A	the management and oversight of allegations against people who work with children
B	providing guidance to employers and voluntary associations about how to deal with allegations against people who work with children
C	Both of the above

Question 8: It How many children in a class of 30 will suffer with some form of mental health issue

A	9
B	3
C	15

Question 9: Which of these may lead to mental health issues in children? Choose as many as you think are correct

A	Poverty
B	Issues and difficulty in school
C	Lack of positive relationships
D	Being a victim of bullying
E	Parental issues – abuse, alcohol/drug issues, parental ill health

Question 10: How many missing children reports are issued to the Police every year?

A	330,000
B	225,000
C	100,000

Remember that we must be vigilant at all times and think that **'it could happen here'**

Please list three words to describe the safeguarding culture below:
1.
2.
3.

Thank you for taking time in completing this survey.

Figure 5.2b

Site walks with your facilities team will allow you to regularly assess the safety of the school site. Always have the worst-case scenario in your head and be thinking, 'it can happen here'. You will need to train your cleaners, your kitchen staff and your wider facilities management team so they are aware of their responsibilities and what to look out for. You should train your exam invigilators, especially as children can be more anxious and stressed in exam season. Children will most likely approach some of these members of staff, and they are also part of your front-line defence in noticing any signs of abuse or neglect.

Quality assurance

Your safeguarding is only as good as what it is like day to day. A true test of this is to see what the school operates like without you there. You will need to build in different methods of quality assurance to test out how safe the school is and how vigilant your staff are. What follows are a few examples of how you may do this.

Governor meeting

Organise a half-term meeting with your safeguarding governor and ask them to come to school prepared with questions. The first couple of meetings you might have to help to train them up in what type of questions they need to ask. After this, though, ask them to come with questions that check the SCR; staff training; the number of children on child protection plans; and also to look at a safeguarding record and to discuss any allegations against staff.

This will reassure them that you are leading safeguarding thoroughly and that you know what you're doing, but it will also prepare them for questions they may get in an OFSTED inspection and skills them up and develops their knowledge of day-to-day safeguarding.

Safeguarding team meeting

Make sure you have a weekly meeting with your safeguarding team or your deputies. Here you can discuss recent cases and any concerns that you have about pupils or their families. You can also use these meetings to train each other up and you should use them to check your record keeping and to quality-assure the work you are doing against your action plan. Take minutes of these meetings so that every week you can check that you have completed any actions that were set.

Random visitor

This is where you ask a colleague from another school to turn up at your school and ask to see you. They can then check your safeguarding procedures for visitors coming to your school. They can feedback on the front of house routines, what they had to fill in, if they were escorted anywhere and they can also make comment on site safety. It's a really useful piece of quality assurance to use with colleagues who visit your school. You can then return the favour the next time you visit their school.

Audits

Normally each year you'll be asked to complete an audit for the Local Authority Safeguarding Partnership, and you may also be asked to do one for your trust or your governors. These are really useful tools to quality assure your work and, again, it can be beneficial to ask an external party to do this on your behalf. From these you can highlight areas of good practice and you can also form action plans to make any areas that weren't as good better over the next year. Never shy away from another person or you and your team completing a review of your work.

I hope this chapter has proved useful and has given you an insight of the day-to-day tasks that a designated safeguarding lead may be faced with. It doesn't cover it all, nor should it. You will learn by doing! I have no doubt it is a challenging role and one that carries huge responsibility, but at the same time that responsibility brings out the best in people and it ensures that your school and its community are safe and can go about its day-to-day business free from harm and in an environment where everyone is looking after everyone else: a true team culture.

Leading inclusion scenario five

Your principal is on a course for the day and, as the next most senior person in the building, you are in charge. You have a designated safeguarding lead with you too, who is an associate member of staff.

A member of the teaching staff brings two pupils to you at the end of break time. They are both very upset and the member of staff is also very anxious and making things slightly more difficult for the children. The member of staff explains that one of the pupils came to them at break time and said that they were worried about their friend, the other pupil in front of you now. The member of staff asks the pupil to explain what happened.

The pupil is upset, and as she starts to explain she gets more upset. She describes a situation where one of the teaching staff, who is on a salaried route and training, has contacted her via social media and they had been chatting. She explains that several explicit photos had been sent. She says she has evidence of these on her phone. She also says that last night they met up in the local park and went for a walk where they ended up taking part in sexual activity. She is really worried about what has happened and while she really likes the member of staff, she knows that the member of staff shouldn't have done what they did. The member of staff is a female teacher who is training via a salaried route and teaches in the same department as the colleague who has brought the pupils to see you.

Think carefully how you would handle this.

- Who would you talk to?
- Who do you HAVE to tell?

- How would you support the pupil?
- How would you investigate the allegation? Think of the steps that you would have to take and what you would also say to the pupils and to the colleague in front of you.
- What would you do with the phone?
- What would be the short-term (immediate) outcome?
- What may be the long-term outcome?

6 Attendance

Leading attendance is one of the most strategic aspects of leading inclusion, and it can be the most challenging. This challenge is due to many external factors that you have limited control over. No matter the catchment of your school, you will have to dedicate time and energy into raising attendance. Poor attendance in a setting is part of a vicious circle of underperformance. The correlation between high attendance and high attainment is strong, so you must dedicate time and resources to improving attendance. With poor attendance comes an increased safeguarding concern too, and you must make home visits to check that children are safe and well.

The impact that you can have on a school and on a community with improved attendance can be hugely significant. Children will achieve more, they will be safer and they will have an internal drive to come to school. As lead of attendance you need to be realistic about your incremental improvements: you can't bring about vast improvements quickly. It's like turning an oil tanker. It takes time and you need to embed your practice. If you make a 1% improvement on attendance in a year for a thousand children, that is an excellent achievement and you need to have this in your mind when setting targets.

Throughout this chapter you will see specific examples of strategies, plans and interventions you can use that will support your attendance drive. The chapter will also look at some of the legal aspects and how you can strategically align your attendance plan with your pupil premium plan. For the scenario at the end, think about how you would develop a whole-school strategy to improve attendance. Use the examples and strategies in the chapter to prompt your thinking about what may or may not work in your setting.

Leading attendance

You have to have a team with you when leading attendance; this is not a one-person job. The size of your team will depend on staffing and your school's budget. You should at the very least have an attendance officer and another associate member of staff. Their jobs will be primarily about recording registers, making phone calls to chase absences, home visits and so on. Back in Chapter 2, we looked at a pastoral structure and how each tier can help you. That structure can be applied to attendance and you can have clear job responsibilities.

Tier 1

Your form tutors are an integral part of leading attendance. They are the ones who see the children every day, and the ones who promote and drive the importance of attendance. They should be monitoring attendance, chasing up absence slips and also making regular phone calls home. In this tier are your teachers, too. They should be taking accurate and timely registers, and ensuring they flag up any absences or patterns of absence.

Tier 2

This group of people support in the day-to-day operations of leading attendance. Each one of your heads of year should be tracking and monitoring the attendance of their groups. They will promote and celebrate attendance within each year group and through the house competition. They should take ownership of their year and lead their tutors. Your safeguarding lead will have a list of vulnerable pupils they will monitor. If children on that list don't arrive at school, it should be flagged straight away, a call and home visit made, and their social worker should be notified. Your behaviour support workers and assistant SENDCO will have groups of children to monitor and track. Make sure that your SENDCO and assistant SENDCO have attendance of their cohort firmly on their improvement plans and liaise with them regularly to evaluate the attendance of SEN children. Attendance of SEN children should play a significant part in their annual reviews.

Tier 3/4

This tier is more strategic, but should play a part in your leadership of attendance, and you must have some form of operational input. You will have a list of pupils who are *persistently absent*, and it is this tier of colleagues who will be having more formal meetings with families in this bracket. Your SENDCO will meet pupils with EHCPs as part of their annual reviews and there may be some children whose attendance is affected by medical conditions. This is where reasonable adjustments must be made.

There used to be a Tier 5 when I first started leading attendance, and that was an education welfare officer. You may be fortunate enough to still work in a Local Authority that employs these. When you work together effectively, there is no better intervention to improve the attendance of hard to reach families than an education welfare officer.

Attendance is referenced a lot in the OFSTED framework, and it will be part of your school improvement plan (SIP). It should cascade down into the plans of your pastoral team and of the SENDCO. If children are experiencing good lessons on a day-to-day basis where they are rewarded, challenged and stretched, they will naturally want to come to school every day. This is why you must get your ethos and inclusive culture right. An unhappy child, who is anxious, nervous and bored, will avoid the thing that is making them feel this way.

Creating an attendance strategy

You must have a clear, concise plan of what you and your team want to achieve throughout the year. You need some SMART targets; these may come from your trust. They are crucial to directing the work of you and your team.

An example of an attendance target from your trust could be 'to ensure that attendance in schools improves quickly and is broadly in line with national figures.' You will need to make sure that this target is in your pastoral development plan, and make sure that your colleagues in Tiers 2 and 3 have this a key performance indicator. They need to analyse data on their cohort and make sure their target is SMART. If they lead a year group whose attendance was 92% the year before, their target should be aspirational and realistic.

As you can see from the strategy in Figure 6.1, there is a clear aim and it is broken down into several areas. One of my leadership principles is to lead positively and generate positive experiences, so you can see I have weighted that area more but included 'encouragement strategies' and, finally, the more punitive ones. A strategy has to have sufficient detail and contain clear lines of accountability.

There is an example in Figure 6.2 of how you can detail this – it has to have clarity about how to measure impact and how your team will quality assure it.

Positive strategies to promote excellent attendance

These are self-explanatory and are designed to embed positive attendance behaviours. Things like certificates, badges and points systems are simple to do, and when done correctly can motivate children to develop a team mentality around

Table one: Key elements of 'Raising attendance levels across the whole school' (FIGURE 6.1)

Strategy	Target group
Improved tracking system and pre-identification of students – (new tracking system)	Whole school
Creation of a one-page attendance summary document – updated weekly to track trends Greater monitoring of work and impact of Attendance lead and pastoral team	Whole school and key groups
Positive student-centred strategies	
1. Certificates for 100% (weekly, half-termly and termly)	Whole school – for individuals at 100%
2. FA Cup	Whole school – by form group
3. Rewards (half-termly, termly) – ice-cream van, trophy and similar (pupil voice)	Whole school – through forms
4. House points	Whole school
5. House cup	Whole school
6. 100% badges	Whole school
7. Positive promotion (display, twitter, weekly assembly, notice boards)	Whole school
8. Heads of Year praise (half-termly certificates)	Whole school
9. Interform competitions per year group	Whole school
10. 96% attendance linked to half termly positive attitude awards	Whole school
Encouragement strategies for students and families	
1. Nudge letters	93-95% group
2. Postcards	93-95% group
3. Head of Year/Student Welfare monitoring (PP pupils)	90-92% group
4. Form tutor monitoring	93-95% group
5. Y11 PP contracts	Pupil Premium previous PA group
6. EWO – home visits	<90% group
7. Deployment of Maltby attendance staff and pastoral teams	Whole school
Discouragement strategies for students and families	
1. <96% attendance – no trips, visits, rewards	All these are at individual student and family level
2. EWO – Fixed Penalty notices	
3. ISAPS	
4. Home visits	
5. Holiday letters/half termly 1,2, 3 letters	
6. Lates – 30-minute detention - daily	

Figure 6.1

Impact measured by:

1. Improvement in overall attendance
2. Improvement in year group and key group attendance
3. Narrowing of gap between Disadvantaged and other students' attendance figures
4. Daily, weekly and half termly analysis of data using new tracking system

Quality assurance and monitoring is completed on a weekly basis in the following ways:

- Attendance data and strategy meeting with VP and Attendance lead.
- Meeting with HOY, SWM, VP and Attendance Lead – review reports are submitted and impact shown against overall attendance figure. Group are all (or mostly) PP. Strategies used are indicated and reviewed.
- Form tutor data is tracked and reported on via spreadsheet to see the impact on attendance
- EWO caseload is reviewed regularly by VP and termly by VP and Associate Principal
- Number of certificates tracked and random QA with student voice done half termly
- Nudge letters and Y11 PP contracts reviewed and tracked by VP to measure impact
- Number of home visits logged and tallied to see if there is an impact on attendance
- New weekly attendance overview sheet will enable key staff to compare and track whole school and cohort data to previous years and national figures. Scrutiny and future work can be targeted according to the data review

All of these strategies will be reviewed and the impact presented to SLT and Trustees as part of their scrutiny to improve attendance.

Evidence

Attainment and progress improve, particularly Yr 11

Daily data figures

Weekly tracking sheets

Form tutor data

Rewards data

League data

Summarised in report to Trustees

Figure 6.2

attendance. Make sure you make reasonable adjustments for children with disabilities and re-set your 100% competitions each week, half term and term.

FA Cup

Put all your form groups into a hat and make a big deal of the draw. In the past I have used the form tutors to do the draws. Make sure you use your social media avenues to help you and create a display board. The idea is that during a school week, one form group takes on another. The group that has the highest attendance goes through to the next round, and after Round 1 you can create a 'plate' competition, so the losers still have something to aim for. You can do two of these per year – make sure you have a big trophy and a good prize at the end.

Year group and form group rewards

There are so many you can do. At the start of each half term I go into each year group's assembly and set a challenge; the year group with the highest attendance for that half term will win a prize. Prizes I have used before have included:

- An ice-cream for EVERY pupil in the winning year group
- A chocolate fountain
- A roller disco
- An obstacle course
- Hot dogs and popcorn
- Movie mornings

Use student voice to help you, and offer a worthy prize. Form group rewards can be driven by your Tier 1 and 2 staff but can include:

- Pizza parties
- Bacon butty and cup of tea mornings
- Hot chocolate treats

Remember to always reset at the end of each week or half term so everyone gets a chance to win.

Encouragement strategies to promote excellent attendance

These are useful and seem non-threatening, so they can help to promote more positive relationships with hard-to-reach families whose children may have poor attendance. They also help to give pupils a direct nudge.

The 90 club

Anything less than 90% puts pupils in the 'persistently absent' bracket, and it is a statistical measure for your school. You need to have as few children in this bracket as you can. We decided that form tutors would track the attendance of children who were just above 90% for a period of time. Each day the pupil ticks off their name on the form outlined in Figure 6.3. If they manage a full week, they are given a 'queue jump' pass for break time and become part of the 90 club. Once this habit was formed over several weeks, pupils moved away from persistent absence and towards a better level of attendance. You can then add or remove children as their attendance rises or falls.

Nudge letters

This idea came from a piece of research that was done by Todd Rogers and Avi Feller. It was written in a blog by Stephen Tierney and is very useful. Their research evidenced a 5-10% improvement in chronic absences, and that most hard-to-reach families may have numeracy and literacy barriers and don't see percentages as an issue; they think that 90% is good. These parents will have issues understanding long letters, and communication needs to be short and simple. The diagrammatic way Rogers and Feller presented data helped parents make the link more than a number would. It was red and green, and made a direct comparison to other children in the class and how school and parents need to work together.

THE 90 CLUB

"The 90 Club" is a mentoring program that helps encourage every student to have a minimum of 90% attendance throughout the year. The Dfe states that **73%** of pupils who have over **95%** attendance achieve **5** or **more** GCSEs at grades 4-9. If your attendance drops below 90%, your tutor will mentor you until your attendance reaches 90% where you will earn a reward and become a member of The 90 Club

Name	Monday	Tuesday	Wednesday	Thursday	Friday

Figure 6.3

We started sending these letters to families whose children were averaging 90-93% attendance so we could 'nudge' them to improve. An example of my letter is shown in the following figure.

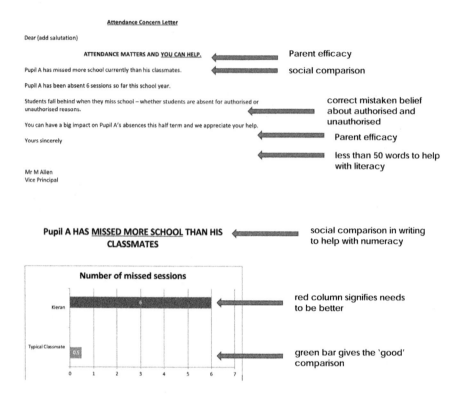

On the second page of the letter was the diagram shown above.

We sent out about 50 of these per half term and saw an improvement in over 30% of the families we targeted.

Thinking point 1

You are head of Year 11, and the cohort's attendance figure for when they were in Year 10 was 91.5%. Think of the strategies that you may use to try and improve on this figure, considering the positive correlation between excellent attendance and attainment. Who would you ask to help?

Jot down your ideas.

Punitive strategies to promote excellent attendance

Some children will be persistently absent from school and they will continue to be throughout the year despite your best interventions. The law states that parents have a legal duty to ensure that their children attend school regularly. If they consistently fail to meet that duty, then there are several punitive approaches you can take.

Where your school is based will determine the steps you need to take with the Local Authority to pursue legal actions. Some trusts have employed their own welfare officers to tackle poor attendance. This can be a very good resource when knocking on doors and chasing concerns. Unfortunately only official education welfare officers have the legal powers to process prosecutions. If you do not have an education welfare officer, you will have to build up evidence to indicate what you have done to try and improve the child's attendance.

A graduated response to attendance

You must demonstrate your evidence of intervention when pursuing legal actions. This is where the graduated response can also support you and your staff. You must have a tiered approach to your attendance strategy, and throughout you need to have letters of increasing severity.

In some Local Authorities you will need to complete an Early Help Assessment to investigate why there is an issue. This assessment could lead to a worker helping the family to improve attendance. They are not an education welfare officer, but a family support worker. Communicate with them regularly, and hold regular meetings to review attendance and the work you are doing. By working together with another agency, you may be able to alleviate some of the barriers and improve attendance.

Examples of the interventions you can use as part of a graduated response are as follows.

Wave One	Wave Two	Wave Three
Form tutor/head of year call	90 club	Education welfare officer caseload/Early Help Assessment worker
Head of year tracking and monitoring	Referral to early help for attendance support	Attendance final warning letter 3
Home visit	Referral to your education welfare officer if you have one	Local Authority attendance panel
Nudge letters	Attendance letter 2	Fixed penalty notice
Nudge postcards	Internal school attendance panel	
Attendance concern and warning letter 1		

OFSTED and your role

Under the heading of behaviour and attitudes in the new OFSTED framework, you will find the following related to attendance and punctuality:[1]

> The judgement focuses on the factors that research and inspection evidence indicate contribute most strongly to pupils' positive behaviour and attitudes,

thereby giving them the greatest possible opportunity to achieve positive outcomes.

These factors are:

- a strong focus on attendance and punctuality so that disruption is minimised

- clear and effective behaviour and attendance policies with clearly defined consequences that are applied consistently and fairly by all staff; children, and particularly adolescents, often have particularly strong concepts of fairness that may be challenged by different treatment by different teachers or of different pupils.

The 'good' descriptor states the following:

- Pupils have high attendance, come to school on time and are punctual to lessons. When this is not the case, the school takes appropriate, swift and effective action.

As leader of attendance you should have all the relevant information to hand. Create an electronic tracking system that indicates your attendance figures for the school and all key groups. Present this data over time, in particular three-year trends. Have your attendance strategy to hand and all the interventions you use. You can show these to the inspector and talk through them. Leave a pack for the inspectors in their base room so they can view all of the information when they choose. A top tip for any OFSTED inspection is to have everything you need ready and with you. If you have to go and find data to answer a question, then it questions your strong focus on attendance.

Present data that shows you have made an impact.

- What groups have improved?
- By how much?
- What is the comparison to national rates?
- What is the comparison to local schools?

Show that you have *demonstrable impact on the attendance of pupils who have particular needs*. This is where you need to show your SEN data and have three or four case studies that detail the intervention and impact a child's attendance. Some examples of what you can produce come next.

An attendance tracker

This spreadsheet (Figure 6.4) gives me all the information I need for the school, including persistent absence, and it is broken down by year group. Things like this save so much time and help when presenting data. I now have a version 2 – always keep adapting your systems.

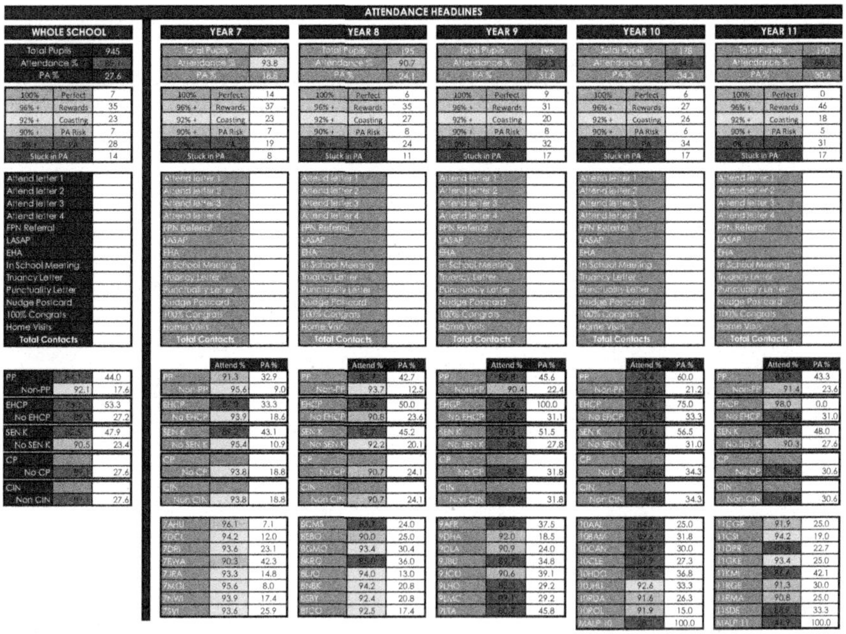

Figure 6.4 Mock-up of a whole school attendance tracker

Case studies

Make these look good and ensure you have your logo, school colours and values on them (Figure 6.5). You can then insert the relevant details, and the intervention and impact of these. Three or four of these indicate you are targeting the right pupils and your work is having the desired effect. As leader of inclusion, I would suggest that you ask your heads of year to have four or five of these per year group.

Key cohorts and groups

Present data on key groups. Make sure you have liaised with your SENDCO and your Pupil Premium Champion for their data. If you are responsible for all of it then make sure your tracker shows it.

Your data has to be clear so that it shows the impact of your work. Figure 6.6 is an example of how I presented my pupil premium attendance data alongside the plan and spending. It was a key area of improvement from our last inspection so I knew it would be scrutinised.

The use of colour is really useful and can tell a visual story; however, it is important to note that in this example, even though there were still attendance gaps (dark grey), the light grey clearly indicates movement, and an improvement of closing the gap by almost 0.4% of a cohort like this is significant. I had my pupil premium plan ready to triangulate everything. Have everything you need to hand.

	Pupil A photo here
Name: **Year:** **DOB:** **SEND:** **PP:** **House:**	

Background information:

Pupil A's school attendance has been poor all the way through school. They started in September 20??, their attendance was 69.5% in Year 7, 39.7% in Year 8 and 29.1% in Year 9. She suffers with extreme anxiety and OCD. They are currently working with CAMHS and are prescribed medication. They have previously been subject to a Child Protection Plan and Early Help have also worked with the family. Despite numerous attempts to re-refer to Early Help, the family refuse. We have implemented a comprehensive graduated approach to try to re-engage Pupil A, including working with CAMHS.

Strategies implemented to support:

- Daily / weekly phone calls and home visits conducted.
- Reduced timetable
- RAG rated timetable
- Hub provision
- Escorted to lesson / Hub
- Accompanied in lesson
- VLN referral
- MAST referral
- CAMHS referral

Positive Impact:

The Attendance Team have held numerous meetings with the family and made several home visits. There is daily contact in periods of absence and a good relationship with parents. There is a clear line of communication between the school and home. Parents are supportive of school and are working closely with both school and CAMHS. Pupil A currently has a reduced timetable and works mostly from The Hub. Recently, they had started to access more lessons, and we were attempting to increase their timetable gradually.

Figure 6.5 Example of description that could be used in a case study

Attendance data

	Other 2016-17	PP 2016-17	Gap	Other 2017-18	PP 2017-18	Gap	change	Yr by Yr
Year 7	95.80%	92.57%	+3.23%	96.25%	92.70%	+3.55%	+0.32	
Year 8	94.33%	92.44%	+1.89%	95.87%	91.94%	+3.93%	+2.04	+0.7
Year 9	94.96%	92.03%	+2.93%	94.30%	91.92%	+2.38%	-0.55	+0.47
Year 10	94.98%	90.43%	+4.53%	94.16%	92.11%	+2.05%	-2.48	-0.88
Year 11	95.90%	91.23%	+4.67%	95.89%	92.42%	+3.47%	-1.27	-1.06
All	95.26%	91.81%	+3.45%	95.31%	92.25%	+3.06%	-0.39	

Figure 6.6 Example data to show impact

Thinking point 2

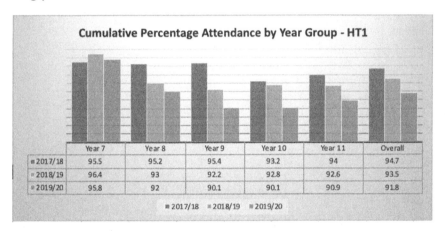

Figure 6.7 Example of data set that can be presented to Governors

Figure 6.7 is the data set you have to present to the governors for the first half term of your new academic year. You are the attendance lead and need to explain this data.

■ What would you take with you?

■ What would you have to present to them at the meeting to indicate you were aware of the issues from the data?

■ What strategic leadership points could you also raise to help you with raising the profile of attendance?

Jot down your answers.

Trust driver group/school-to-school support

One of the things that works really well in my current role is that we have a driver group for attendance. It consists of the key inclusion leads for each of the three schools and the attendance lead for the trust. The group has a clear remit to use research and excellent practice to develop systematic approaches across all the academies to improve attendance. I am a big advocate for inviting others to your setting and asking them to review your practice. They give an objective account and also suggest excellent improvement strategies.

Can you join up with another local school or another school in your trust to work together to look at your attendance practice?

Leading inclusion scenario six

You have taken up a new role as vice principal at a large secondary school. There has previously not been a leader with specific responsibilities for inclusion. During your first half term you are inspected by OFSTED, and they are clear that attendance at your school is not good enough and neither are your systems to monitor them. The inspector clearly indicates concern around the attendance differences of disadvantaged pupils to their peers and for pupils with an EHCP. One of the things they identify the school has to improve on is the following:

Insist that regular attendance from all students is the norm, by:

- Monitoring trends in the attendance of individuals and groups of students
- Working closely with students and families to overcome the barriers to full attendance
- Demonstrating clear strategic thinking to overcome barriers for disadvantaged pupils and those with additional needs

Draw up a strategic plan that demonstrates how you will tackle this area for improvement. In the plan, identify what actions you will take and what interventions you will use. You also need to identify how you will quality assure your work and measure any associated impact.

Note

1 OFSTED School Inspection Handbook, Department for Education, November 2019

Chapter 6 references

Rogers, T., and Feller, A. (2017). *Intervening Through Influential Third Parties: Reducing Student Absences at Scale via Parents*. Harvard University via the Leading Learner Blog. https://leadinglearner.me/2017/07/02/absences-matter-and-you-can-help/

7 Pupil premium

Research by the Education Endowment Foundation in their report entitled *The Attainment Gap* (2017) indicated that children who come from disadvantaged backgrounds will generally be behind their peers academically, socially and emotionally. By the end of their secondary education, this gap could be as large as 19.3 months. Schools have benefited from huge amounts of money given to narrow the attainment gap between disadvantaged pupils and their peers.

Every school has its own challenges, but whatever they are, we have to work strategically and plan to spend this funding to narrow this gap. We cannot simply let children who are disadvantaged continue to fall behind. Some schools have accomplished amazing things, and we should celebrate their success and use their ideas. This chapter will focus on some of these ideas and work from the Education Endowment Foundation, and I will focus on my ideas and experiences from a time when our school, with a 58% disadvantaged cohort, closed the attainment gap.

Pupil premium eligibility

Government guidance states that, to be classed as pupil premium or disadvantaged, a child needs to meet any of these criteria (funding from April 2020 included):

- A pupil who has ever been recorded as 'free school meals' eligible in the last six years, known as 'Ever 6'. The current funding per pupil in this criterion is £955.

- A LAC. The current funding for this criterion is £2345.

- Children who have ceased to be 'Looked After' because of adoption, a special guardianship order, a child arrangement order or a residence order. The current funding for this criterion is £2345.

- Recorded as an 'Ever 6' service child, or in receipt of a child pension from the Ministry of Defence. The current funding for this criterion is £310.

Until recently we all had funds for Year 7 literacy and numeracy catch up, but the government has cut this funding due to the implementation of their Fair Funding Formula, and as I write, the government has announced a £1 billion budget to help children catch up because of the COVID-19 pandemic. I am sure we will have to plan for, report on and measure the impact of this funding in the near future. As with all funding, though, we welcome it and will try and use it to support our disadvantaged children.

This next part of the chapter will focus on the support, research and ideas that are out there to help you and your disadvantaged children. You will find links to web pages, specific ideas and inserts of research that has been provided to senior leaders. Use the research when planning your spending, but as I have said throughout the book, have your setting and children always at the forefront of your thinking.

Education Endowment Foundation (EEF)

The EEF is a charity that started to use academic research to provide useful information that senior leaders could use to support their disadvantaged learners. One of the most useful and widely used pieces of research produced was their toolkit (2011). The toolkit uses live data from schools and academic research to signpost and evaluate interventions that are used to support disadvantaged learners. One of the most useful parts of the toolkit is the evaluation section. It gives a breakdown on the impact the intervention could have with your children, and it gives justification as to why you want to include it within your plan and spending.

The diagram gives you an indicator of the potential cost and the evidence strength (number of locks), and it gives a sign of the potential months gain that it could generate with your children. Read all of these and make reference to them throughout your plan and when you present your ideas and spending to your governing body.

Further research by the EEF in 2019 was titled the *Pupil Premium Guide*. The guide gives further recommendations to senior leaders and it is a really useful document to use when planning your interventions. It recommends a tiered approach to spending and gives clarity on what the priorities of your spending should be. This research triangulates well with the graduated response document I discussed earlier in the SEN chapter, and it also promotes *quality-first teaching* as the main priority to support the learning of disadvantaged pupils.

The priorities highlighted in the guide are:

1. Teaching – to focus funding and time on training staff, and making sure they are supported to help your disadvantaged pupils.

2. Targeted support for pupils – to make sure that you plan for the right type of support for your pupils.

3 Non-academic factors – to think about the impact of poor attendance, behaviour and attitudes of pupils, and the social and emotional support they may need.

You can see all these documents and more by accessing the EEF website (www.educationendowmentfoundation.org.uk).

To make your plan effective and close the gap, you should work with other leaders and your community to identify what barriers your children face. Your pupils may face different challenges from others, and it is important you plan specifically to overcome these.

Barriers to learning for disadvantaged pupils

The setting you work in and the community you serve will dictate the barriers to learning that your disadvantaged learners may face. In general, the more disadvantaged your community is, the more pupil premium children you will have and the more barriers they may have to overcome. No matter what the type or the number of barriers there are, it is your job as a senior leader of inclusion not to allow any adult in school to lower their expectations of your disadvantaged cohort. This can be one of the most damaging approaches. We do not make it an excuse to lower our expectations of our children.

Our job is to help them to overcome these barriers, and we should expect exactly the same level of work from them as their non-disadvantaged peers. If you are currently the pupil premium lead in your school, or part of the team that leads on it, one of the first things you must do is identify these barriers. Create a working group, and in that group make sure you have pastoral leaders, attendance officers, some form tutors and, if possible, any members of staff who live in the community. Each one of these will bring valuable insights, challenges and support when determining the barriers your children face. Once you have identified these, they will give you a framework to utilise the research and to strategically plan your approach.

Some of the barriers you may identify are:

- Low attendance – we discussed in previous chapters the strong correlation between good attendance and high attainment

- Low aspiration

- Lack of enrichment or 'cultural capital'

- Lack of opportunity

- Readiness for learning and engagement – this could be cognitive related, equipment related or SEND related. You will need to test these out and also use your evidence from graduated responses

- Safeguarding issues

- Behaviour issues – particularly related to SEMH needs
- Historic academic underperformance

Once you have got your key barriers identified, you need to share them with staff. Everyone has to be aware and everyone has to be working to overcome them. Pupil premium strategies cannot be a bolt-on. Remember to re-iterate the first tier of the *Pupil Premium Guide* and explain the importance of Quality-First Teaching and how you can support your staff here with effective CPD. You need to ensure that the staff knows the barriers, knows who the children are and, by following a well-structured and consistent framework, delivers good lessons.

Thinking point 1

Reflect on your current setting, or a previous one.

- What are/were the main barriers that children face(d)?
- How do you or did you overcome these?
- Was there, or is there, a plan drawn up?
- Did the strategies work?
- How do you, or did you, know?

Jot your answers down.

The pupil premium plan

There is an OFSTED requirement that you publish your plan on your website and that it must detail your spending. You must make sure that you include all the relevant details and, in this plan, highlight your barriers and what you are going to spend money on to overcome them.

There are lots of plans out there and a lot of schools use formats that are produced by the government, a union or a pupil premium based organisation, like the EEF. I used an amalgamation of these and wanted to include all of the key financial information alongside the barriers that we had identified. This was to help governors, teaching staff and leaders easily reference key interventions, and it also enabled me to add quarterly reviews to the same document.

An example plan

This section of the chapter will give you some examples of how I wrote our plan and how I linked it all together. You can write your plan however you want, so long as you include the key information and how you are going to spend money. It is important that you find a style you prefer, and that the report makes it easy for you write and regularly review it. Our plan and what I discuss can be a guide and an example of how you may decide to write it (Figure 7.1). In my settings we have had significant pupil premium budgets and therefore I felt the need to have a detailed plan that reflected the level of spending and the impact we were having.

Barriers

This section is where you identify all the work you may have done with your working group. I used it as an area to highlight any strengths or weaknesses from the previous year, and how we would address them. I grouped them into the OFSTED framework headings. It makes sense to do this as you can strategically link your development plan to your pupil premium plan, and it enables everyone to see the joined-up approach you are taking. It also allows you to highlight some of the pertinent data which reinforces why you are planning the interventions in the document. Figure 7.2 is an example of this.

Pupil Premium is additional funding given to schools, to enable them to support disadvantaged pupils, maximise their progress and close the attainment gap between them and their peers. A key challenge for the school to support students who are eligible for Pupil Premium funding. Our priority is to ensure that all disadvantaged students, including those who are performing well, are supported and challenged by adopting a much personalised approach to ensure that their progress and attainment is maximised. The DfE has no particular view on using the Pupil Premium funding on whole-school initiatives as long as the progress and attainment gap is closing between the highest and lowest achieving pupils, within a school context of generally improving attainment. The DfE and Ofsted are unanimous in their belief that Pupil Premium funding can be spent 'where school leaders feel it is most needed' as long as every effort is taken to ensure that all students, regardless of their background or ability, is given the opportunity to excel academically.

Summary Financial Information

Local Authority Secondary School (11-16)	
Academic Year	
Total number of pupils	1007
Number of pupils eligible for Pupil Premium	536
Percentage of Ever6/LAC/Service	53.22%
Total budget allocated from the DFE	£485,495
Total budget allocated for Pupil Premium	£575,711
Date of most recent Pupil Premium review	
Date for next internal review of this strategy	

Figure 7.1

Quality of Teaching and Learning	Last year's plan identified several strategies that had demonstrable impact on the quality of Teaching and Learning for PP children. These strategies also significantly developed PP children's level of literacy, specifically their reading and spelling ages. Quality assurance of this work and further embedding is needed this year to bring about further improvements. The GRIT five part lesson will be used throughout school alongside other strategies to improve the literacy levels of Key Stage 3 children and the outcomes of Key Stage 4 children. Effective use of data in planning that requires staff to focus on six PP children in each class they teach will sharpen our approach to the teaching and learning of PP children. Seminars and CPD seminars have been introduced to support this work. Research from the EEF is highlighted in these sessions and weekly as part of the staff bulletin.
Personal Development, Behaviour and Safety	A significant proportion of our PP spend is allocated to wrap around care. A plethora of work is being done to support PP pupils around attendance, mental well-being, reduction of Fixed Term Exclusions and positive learning. Data-driven reports are used to highlight areas of strength and when further intervention is required. Communication between pastoral staff and all stakeholders is a key aspect of making improvements. All members of the pastoral team are identifying and intervening to improve the attendance of PP children in school. A more detailed strategic approach to monitoring attendance is being used and PP funds have been allocated to increasing the amount of support from our Education Welfare Officer. A new strategy for rewarding excellent attendance has been implemented.
Student Outcomes	As indicated in the Leadership and Management description above there are clear areas for this plan to address in relation to outcomes. Please make reference to these above. One of our key areas to focus on is narrowing the Progress gap between PP children and their peers. The current gaps can be seen below.

	Other		PP		
Area	2015-2016	2016-2017	2015-2016	2016-2017	Gap +/-
Progress 8	-0.16	-0.09	-0.60	-0.53	Same
Attainment 8	37.45	43.82	33.0	34.64	Grown by 4.73
English element attainment	8.12	9.92	7.17	7.82	Grown by 1.15
Maths element attainment	9.29	8.99	7.38	7.09	Reduced by 0.01
Open element attainment	14.01	14.29	10.65	12.24	Reduced by 1.31
Basics 4+	65.6%	64.6%	41.7%	43.6%	Reduced by 2.9%
Basics 5+	17.8%	47.8%	16.7%	24.5%	Grown by 23.3%

Figure 7.2

Desired outcomes

I really feel this section is a good introduction to the work in the plan and it sets the scene in a clear and concise way. It also gives you the chance to celebrate areas of success. Directly following this section was my 'barriers to learning' and then what my **desired outcome** of the plan was, alongside the success criteria (Figure 7.3). These are your crucial statements that underpin your plan, and the work you and your colleagues will undertake.

Once you have these, your plan can be split up into each desired outcome, what you will spend the money on and its impact. If I take Desired Outcome C, you can see how I then planned to meet the success criteria (Figure 7.4).

I always find it useful to start with a table; that way you can track the impact of your work much more easily. Add quarterly reviews – this is where I present the plan and the data against the success criteria. It allows governors to quality assure the work and ensure the spending was impactful. It allows them the opportunity to

	In-school barriers (issues to be addressed in school, such as poor literacy skills)
A	PP pupils come to school with weak literacy skills
B	PP pupils lack the resilience and determination to complete work
C	PP pupils come to school less prepared than their peers and this impacts on their equipment and homework completion.
	External barriers (issues which also require action outside school, such as low attendance rates)
D	Attendance of PP pupils is lower than their peers therefore having an impact on their progress

	Desired outcomes (desired outcomes and how and when they will be measured)	Success criteria
A	To narrow the attainment and progress gaps of PP pupils vs their peers	Attainment and progress gap narrows
B	To improve the attainment and progress of Mid/High PA PP pupils	Attainment and progress of this cohort improves
C	To improve the attendance of PP pupils	Attendance gap to other is narrowed
D	To continue to provide wrap-around care and support for PP pupils	Ensuring PP pupils have access to required support from internal and external agencies to improve their attendance and their progress.

Figure 7.3

Desired Outcome C : To improve the attendance of PP pupils

Attendance of PP students improved XX. PP Vs NPP gap reduced to XX.

Measure		Start Mar	SP4 Apr	SP5 June	SP6 July	Outcome July / Aug
PP attendance	Target	N/A				
	Actual	93.06%	93.14%	92.66%		
PP Vs NPP attendance gap	Target	N/A				
	Actual	-2.95%	-2.89%	-3.04%		
PP Persistent absence	Target	N/A				
	Actual	11.41%	10.92%	12.35%		
PP Vs NPP Persistent absence	Target	N/A				
	Actual	-6.43%	-6.63%	-7.97%		

Review 1 There has been a positive shift in the attendance of PP pupils and this has increased by nearly a full percent since this time last year. The strategies to support the attendance of PP pupils have shown impact but there is still room for improvement. Persistent absence is still an issue.

Review 2 While the attendance figure has dropped slightly we have still reduced the PP v non-PP gap by over half a percent since last year indicating the strategies put in place have had an impact. Work needs to continue next year and the re-structuring of the pastoral and attendance teams will do this. PA is still high, however, when compared with the national figure for PP PA which is 22% we can see our figure is way below. However, it still needs reducing and particularly the gap between PP and non-PP PA. The work of our EWO will target this next year.

Figure 7.4

ask challenging questions and to ask for evidence that you are improving outcomes for disadvantaged children.

Once you have the table in place, you can then start to add weight to your plan. Under each outcome, identify specific interventions or strategies that you are going to use. Make sure you add a brief explanation so that other leaders understand what the intervention is and its purpose in the plan. Work closely with your business manager and get a line-by-line breakdown of the funding and what you are spending it on. Make sure to add links to the EEF toolkit (Figure 7.5).

The budget and spending

The chosen approach highlights what you are doing and why, and you can see how I allocated the budget and suggested an intended impact. The review section allows you to monitor and highlight your progress. Finally, the governors' role is to ensure that our spending is cost effective. If you are spending a high percentage of your budget on an unsuccessful intervention, then you should be challenged on that and you may need to make the decision about whether to make changes.

A lot of your budget will already be taken up with staffing, and you must account for this and follow the same process as outlined earlier. It is not good enough to just lump hundreds of thousands of pounds on staffing without a breakdown. You can allocate it to certain staff, e.g., your pastoral and welfare team. Don't be scared to allocate a certain percentage of their salary if they are only involved some of the time. You can allocate some of the costing to running a provision for children.

If you are putting a significant amount of money into pastoral care and your attendance, behaviour and exclusions for disadvantaged children are not where they should be, then your work is not effective. Allocating funds to a provision that has

Chosen Approach	Allocated budget	Review	Intended Impact	Cost effective	Actual spend to date
Pupil Premium Attendance contracts 16 pupils were PA in Y10 and behind in their studies. They are to be given half termly contracts to improve their attendance and to prevent them from being PA pupils again. All are in Y11 and all are disadvantaged. The aim is to improve their attendance, improve communication with home and ultimately improve their progress and attainment.	£4,000	Review of attendance taken to Governors Challenge Board. 5 out of 15 pupils are not in PA – 33% improvement on last year 7 out of 15 are in PA – 54% improvement on last year 3 are EHE or withdrawn. This time last year average attendance of the group was 83.3% It is now 86.5% - 3.2% increase.	To ensure this group of children do not have the same poor level of attendance in Y11. Reduced number of the group who are PA. EEF Toolkit – Parental Engagement (+3) Mentoring (0)	In part – 4 of the 15 stayed out of PA. 5 out of the 15 improved their attendance from the previous year.	
Education Welfare Support In the last OFSTED monitoring visit it was identified that the attendance of PP pupils is a cause for concern in relation to their peers. EWO contract has been extended by a further 2 days to target the attendance of PP pupils. This means we now have a full time 5 days a week EWO.	£26,193	EWO has supported this work and has been proactive in supporting the school. This resource has been well used and has clear impact and will be renewed for next year.	The attendance gap between PP and other to be narrowed. To ensure our PA children have the correct support and Local Authority prosecution is utlisied to boost attendance figures of PP children and reduce PA. EEF Parental Engagement (+3)	Yes – attendance gap between PP and other has reduced and PP has increased.✓	

Figure 7.5

Pastoral Care	Non-teaching
Work of the pastoral teams is crucial in supporting our PP cohort. The team works to support the attendance, behaviour and progress of all PP pupils in their cohorts. Specific work around reducing the number of on-calls and Fixed Term Exclusions of PP pupils in to be undertaken by the Inclusion Lead	HOY (£132,332) Bridge/E&E provision (£78,307) Assistant Principal 0.52 (£37,078) Inclusion Lead 0.52 (£24,552)

Figure 7.6

impact is a much better way to support your children. This way you can show that the provision supports your children, and you can present case studies of success to your governors or OFSTED. Our example is shown in Figure 7.6.

Work closely with your business manager and split the funding into each intervention, and you will also be able to allocate funds for one-off interventions like my attendance contracts in Figure 7.5.

Staff expertise and drive

Your staff body is a key asset to use. To ensure that all staff are aware of my plan, I ask them if they would like to plan an intervention or research project to work with disadvantaged children. They produce a rationale, costings and a projected impact statement. As a leader you can also build this into their performance management. Colleagues who are on Upper Pay Scale (UPS) will have to show the impact of their work at a whole school or year group level, and a project like this will allow them to meet this expectation. You can also award bursary projects for staff to sign up for. You could offer a nominal amount for a colleague to run a research project around one of your desired outcomes. If their plan and idea is worthwhile, they would get the funding and the go-ahead. They must review their work quarterly and measure any impact.

By writing your plan this way and incorporating quarterly reviews, it gives you the necessary evidence and data to allow you to write a detailed pupil premium review of the year's spending. There is nothing worse than having to get historical data and asking people for a review of something they did months ago. Use the plan properly and this will save you lots of time. This annual review of your spending has to be done and published on your website. You can upload the plan; the reviews are a part of it, and a simple one-page summary can highlight your successes and areas to focus on further.

A research project example: using angling as a driver to change behaviour

In a previous setting, one colleague approached me to do some angling on weekly basis. He was an angling coach and wanted to take disadvantaged boys whose behaviour was causing problems and use fishing to build relationships and to mentor them. He needed £2500 for equipment and licences. I thought it was a great idea and he was going to use it to motivate them more in lessons. When we reviewed his work, all of the boys' attendance had improved and their removes from lessons had reduced by 27%; one boy was never removed from a lesson again. Your staff is your biggest and best asset; use them in the plan. They will come up with great ideas that work, and they will help improve outcomes for children.

Thinking point 2

Reflect on your current staff body.

- How many of your colleagues would come up with an idea to work with pupil premium children?
- What type of work would pupils in your school need according to the barriers you have identified earlier?
- How would you lead on this work – what methods of presentation and recruitment could you use?

Jot down your ideas.

The important of effective teaching and learning

The last part of this chapter will look at what we are all professionally trained in teaching, learning and the pedagogy around it.

When referring to the EEF toolkit, pedagogical strategies such as *mastery*, *metacognition*, *collaborative learning* and others have a seriously positive impact on narrowing the attainment gap of pupil premium children to their peers. The Sutton Trust (2011) identified the impact that a good teacher had on a disadvantaged pupil, and the research identified that the average student makes 40% more progress with good teaching as opposed to poor teaching. It is crucial as leaders in disadvantaged settings that our teachers are delivering consistently good lessons. A disadvantaged pupil can make 50% LESS PROGRESS than an average student with poor teaching, whereas if teaching is highly effective for disadvantaged pupils, progress can be increased to 150% of the average progress (Figure 7.7).

As a senior leader in a previous setting, our OFSTED report highlighted that we had an attainment gap that was widening. We adopted a simple but effective

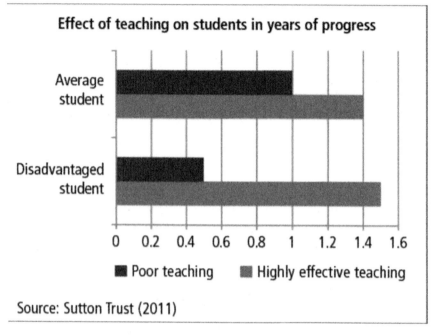

Figure 7.7

teaching and learning model that utilised simple pedagogical approaches that supported the needs of all children's learning. The approach was part of the pupil premium plan and it had a huge impact on the standard of lessons being delivered in the school and the amount of learning that was going on.

The outcomes for Year 11 pupils significantly increased that year; our disadvantaged cohort increased their attainment by the equivalent of a quarter of a grade in every subject, resulting in narrowing the progress gap to zero. At our next OFSTED inspection, the lead HMI (Her Majesty's Inspector) made the following statement about our pupil premium work:

> Senior leaders have radically re-designed their approach to improving the outcomes disadvantaged pupils achieve. The recommendations from an external review of the school's use of the Pupil Premium have been used wisely by senior leaders and their plans are comprehensive and ambitious.

Our vice principal for teaching and learning led this work. It was called *GRIT* and it was a five-part lesson that build on the following principles:

Step 1: Developing Literacy Skills
Step 2: Asking Challenging Questions
Step 3: Modelling High Expectations
Step 4: Maximum Expectations (M.E.) Time and Differentiation for All
Step 5: Consolidating Learning

Step 1: developing literacy skills

This step required staff to include at the start of every lesson a task or tasks that developed pupils' literacy. This could be as simple as a spelling test, or a set of key terms and their definitions that would be used in the lesson. We also then adapted this to include some *recall* skills from previous learning and we called it 'Skills Drill'. As part of our marking policy, we also asked staff to include any previous spelling mistakes in the pupil's book and they would correct these in this time.

Step 2: asking challenging questions

We were aware that our questioning in lessons wasn't challenging enough and didn't require enough thought from our pupils, so this step looked at developing questioning using wrapper questions.

An example of a history question could be:

Why do you think Henry VIII changed the church?

We asked staff to think how they could use a wrapper question to get more depth out of the pupils.

The wrapper prompt could therefore be:

I'm looking for at least three reasons. You have one minute to write down your reasons and before I choose two or three of you to give me the answers.

This approach gives a minimum target, a time frame and a clear indication of how many pupils would be asked to contribute.

A science example could be:

If you wanted to test for hydrogen sulphide gas, what might you do?

The wrapper part would then be:

You need to use between 20 and 60 words and two of these words must be' gas jar'.

This part of the lesson also proved to be the *hook* or the *engage* section, as staff used it to drive the interest of pupils for the upcoming lesson.

Step 3: modelling high expectations

This section was simply for the teacher to do what they do best: to use their knowledge, their pedagogy and skills to model an answer or piece of work for the class. This would be a WAGOLL (What A Good One Looks Like). It ensured that pupils gained confidence in the lesson as they could see and be taken through an example that detailed the content, the length and the structure for their upcoming work. We also used WALK AND TALK approaches with our Key Stage 4 children in this step. They would then be set a similar task during the next step of the lesson.

Step 4: M.E. time and differentiation for all

M.E. time was a simple concept. It was a significant part of the lesson where the class was expected to work hard, independently. They would be told how much work was expected of them during M.E. time. In this step we asked staff to ensure that they 'taught to the top' and then scaffolded the learning down with differentiated strategies that could be by task, by outcome or by behaviour for learning. Staff were encouraged to use strategies such as:

- Sentence stems
- Writing frames
- Mark schemes
- Different levels of questions
- Tests
- Extended writing
- Whatever the colleague felt was appropriate

This period of hard work and focus was significant in the output and understanding of our disadvantaged pupils. It also allowed staff the chance to move around the room and support pupils on a 1:1 or small group basis and incorporate live marking. We made sure that staff were aware of who their pupil premium children were in each lesson and, using the EEF toolkit, asked them to plan to support these pupils via 1:1 work (+5 on the toolkit) or in small groups (+4).

Step 5: consolidating learning

This was the active plenary part of the lesson. We were clear that there had to be a piece of reflective work and staff were asked to produce word webs, recap questions and word walls, and were encouraged to use oracy strategies to get pupils discussing what they had learned in the lesson.

We ensured that we dedicated significant CPD time to this new approach and used other colleagues in the school to model their practice and share how they do things. It was a piece of work that was welcomed by staff and they immediately saw the benefits.

From a behaviour and pastoral point of view, my team noticed a lot less removes from lessons for distracting others or immature behaviour. Pupils were focused and worked hard in lessons. We saw a spike at times during M.E. time as some pupils voted with their feet, but we overcame that by ensuring they completed their

M.E. time work in another room. Through consistent application, it became the norm to deliver this way and our children really grabbed hold of it.

We used each step as part of our quality assurance and performance management cycle. Staff were no longer observed for a lesson and graded; they had five drop-ins through the year, performed by either a senior leader, their line manager or another colleague; and we shared all the good practice we saw at weekly teaching and learning briefings.

This piece of work was a significant piece in the jigsaw puzzle of improving outcomes for our pupils and it fully reinforced the research findings of the EEF about the need for good teaching to support the progress of disadvantaged pupils.

I hope you have found this chapter compelling and that it has given you some ideas about how to structure a pupil premium plan and what you may look to include. In a setting where you are faced with high numbers of disadvantaged children, you really cannot do little projects that will narrow the attainment gap. If you have hundreds of children who are classed as disadvantaged, then the best way you can support their needs is to introduce strategies and interventions that target *every* child in the school. That way you get consistency and routine.

Remember that there are no quick wins, and that part of your strategy should be to ensure that teachers deliver good lessons on a daily basis. When a government gives substantial amounts of money to a school budget, you can rest assured that during an inspection the team will want to speak with you and will want to scrutinise your plan, its impact and your spending. The methods I have outlined in this chapter have passed those tests, and they gave me the detail and clear evidence to indicate what a good job we were doing.

Leading inclusion scenario seven

You have been a member of your senior leadership team for one year and your school is given an inadequate rating by OFSTED in your latest inspection. Your head teacher has asked you to become Pupil Premium Champion for the school and tackle the key areas raised by the inspection.

These are as follows:

- Too many disadvantaged pupils do not come to school often enough.

- Disadvantaged pupils do not get the support they need in the classroom to achieve well.

- Although disadvantaged pupils are now making improved progress, there are still significant gaps between their achievement and the achievement of others. Governors should rigorously hold leaders to account for the use and impact of the additional funds that the school receives.

- The progress of disadvantaged pupils in core subject areas is well below the level it should be, and the effect is that disadvantaged pupils do not achieve an outcome in these subjects in line with what they should.

Reflect on this chapter and what you have learned from previous ones, and write an action plan that clearly addresses the steps you would take to tackle each area outlined in preparation for your next monitoring visit.

Chapter 7 research and references

The Education Endowment Foundation. (2017). *The Attainment Gap.* https://educationendowmentfoundation.org.uk/public/files/Annual_Reports/EEF_Attainment_Gap_Report_2018_-_print.pdf

The Education Endowment Foundation. (2019). *Pupil Premium Guide.* www.educationendowmentfoundation.org.uk/public/files/Publications/Pupil_Premium_Guidance.pdf

The Education Endowment Foundation Toolkit. (2011). www.educationendowmentfoundation.org.uk/evidence-summaries/teaching-learning-toolkit/

The Sutton Trust. (2011). *Improving the Impact of Teachers on Pupils Achievement in the UK – Interim Findings.* https://www.suttontrust.com/wp-content/uploads/2019/12/2teachers-impact-report-final-1.pdf

8 Alternative provision

This chapter will give you an insight of how to strategically plan for an offer of alternative provision for your children. Think about your curriculum offer and whether it fully meets the needs of your children. If you have a group of children who are demotivated and displaying poor behaviour despite several interventions, you will need to consider alternative provision.

This chapter will give you some examples of internal provisions that I have been part of, and how we used our building and our staff to create an alternative pathway. It will cover service level agreements with external providers and make you think about value for money and the correct outcomes for your children. This chapter will look at the different types of alternative provision and it will give an insight in how to strategically plan for creating your own. It will also look at how you can ensure you support your pupils fully when they are accessing alternative provision.

Alternative provision rationale

Alternative provision has become a key strategic intervention for leading inclusion over the past few years. Alternative provision has always been a provision to think about, but its use in the past has been questionable. People saw it as a provision where all the worst-behaved children went, such as in a Pupil Referral Unit, or a place to send children with too complex needs for leaders to plan for. Alternative provision is and can be so much more. School leaders are now seeing the benefit that alternative provision actually brings to pupils.

Some of our children may need a different setting for a period of time, for a day or two, or even full time. One of the key decisions that you will have to make is weighing up the benefit for the child against the cost for the school. We should be using alternative provision to support our children.

Before we look at creating an alternative provision or sourcing one for a pupil or group of pupils, we need to determine what alternative provision actually is.

> Alternative provision is the educational provision arranged by Local Authorities, trusts and schools for pupils who because of exclusion, illness or other reasons would not be able to access suitable educational provision.

Exclusions and alternative provision

In recent years, especially across the secondary setting, we have seen a huge spike in the number of fixed-term and permanent exclusions. There are lots of reasons for this; some are as follows:

- New leadership teams making a stand in a school where behaviour has been historically poor
- New zero-tolerance behaviour systems that escalate behaviours quickly
- Challenging and unmet needs of children in the setting
- Lack of expertise, staff skill or structure in a setting
- Contextualised behaviour challenges

Whatever the reason for the increase in exclusions, the knock-on effect has been an increase in the use of alternative provision, mainly after legal tolerance levels have been met for permanent exclusions or the issuing of a permanent exclusion for a 'one-off' serious incident.

In recent years I have noticed a significant increase in the number of children with an unmet SEMH need that has caused substantial challenges in schools. I have worked in settings where we have struggled to manage these needs and had little specialist support to help. On the back of this spike, we have seen waiting lists for the Child and Adolescent Mental Health Service (CAMHS) grow exponentially, meaning a child may not get specialist support for over two years. There are also more instances of pupils not attending school on medical grounds, as medical professionals are suggesting the school is the cause of their health issues. Sadly the quick way, and more often than not the only way, to get this support has been through exclusions.

As the strategic lead for inclusion, you need to foresee this as much as you can. Use the systems we discussed in Chapter 4 to help and work closely with your SENDCO. There will always be a need for some form of alternative provision for some pupils. It is our job to either create this provision or to source it. Either way the funding has to be there to support the needs of these children.

Thinking point one

Reflect on your own setting and your own trust or Local Authority.

- What alternative provision is there currently on offer? Do you use any?
- What is its value to the child?
- Is it effective? How do you know?
- Is it cost effective?
- How do you track attendance, progress and monitor safeguarding at the provision?

Jot down your ideas.

Creating your own internal provision

In my experience, this is an absolute winner. It allows you to shape a provision that meets the specific needs of your children, and it can be established with your ethos and values. You can use your own staff and with a location based in your setting; with familiar people, you are already alleviating some of the anxieties children would face with attending an external provision.

One thing you must have in your mind is the cost. This is expensive. Schools have developed lots of examples of their own provisions and these can be very successful, but they come at a cost, and in the current funding climate, you will need to draw up a strong strategy to convince leaders in your school to create your own.

Think about how you can work with your SENDCO: if your children are successful in being awarded an EHCP, you can use some of the funding to help support the cost of the provision, especially if it is directly meeting the needs of the children. This funding, your plan and the resulting provision could then become a specialist setting for children in your area.

Before you start to properly plan your idea of an internal provision, you need to think carefully about the following:

- Your ethos/values and how these will run through the provision

- The benefits – why do it? How will it support the pupils? What will be the knock-on effects for them? For future cohorts? What will be the benefits for the school? For your community?

- The location – where will it be in your school?

- The number of pupils who will access it and their year group

- Your graduated response and support – at what point will they meet the threshold and who makes the decision?

- Staffing – how many staff will you need? Who will run it day to day? How do you create the job descriptions?

- Cost – break it down into sub-sections: staffing, resources, curriculum time/cost

- Curriculum – what will they study? Taught by whom? Do they access mainstream classes too? How does it fit in term of school outcomes and baskets? What will be the impact on headline measures?

These topics and areas will form part of your strategic plan, and they will add significant weight to your proposal. Make sure you spend enough time on answering them all, and go and speak to key people in the school – your business manager, your SENDCO, your pastoral team.

Let's address a few of the key areas now, and delve a little deeper into what is required and why they are so important to address.

Ethos/values

An internal provision must be promoted and 'sold' in the right way. You need to make sure that it is reflective of your inclusive ethos and you need to promote it to staff and your community as what it is: a provision that has been created to **support** the needs and the education of your pupils.

Think carefully about the language you use when setting it up and when promoting it with all stakeholders. This is such a key part of the process – the ethos and the environment you create within your provision will either make or break it. It has to start well and be perceived as a supportive and purposeful provision. Think about words such as 'inclusive', 'aspirational', 'tailored', 'purposeful', 'supportive', 'personalised'.

All members of your school community need to be aware of what it is. It is your job as inclusion lead to drive this. Make sure you let staff see the provision when it is being designed and when it's running – invite parents and other pupils into the area so they can see it during the day.

In the provisions I have either set up or helped to oversee, we have always thought carefully about the name for the provision. This can really support your work.

A provision that was a satellite one, shared between schools, we called 'The Lodge'. Children would access it for a few weeks, get the support they needed and then they were slowly re-integrated back into their setting.

The other two provisions I have been involved with were called:

Ethos and Engagement – this reflected the nature of the provision, and the school and my ex-colleague named it when she was designing the provision. It gave a clear message that the provision would support pupils' needs but would be about working hard.

Eleos – the new version of this provision was revamped and called 'Eleos'. This name sat with other Greek names that the school and trust used, Eleos being the goddess of compassion and clemency.

Location/cost/staffing/numbers

The location of your provision is really important, and this could also be a factor that prevents you from setting up your own provision. If you haven't got the space, then you may not be able to set one up.

There are a few questions that you need to consider, too.

- Where is the best place to locate it logistically? By that I mean for access, for toilets and for suitability. Ask your team for their views.

- Can you get the children involved? The more buy-in from them, the better. If you are lucky enough to have buildings within your grounds, you could utilise these, but again that is more cost! Both our provisions within the school building had designated classrooms, a 'break-out' space and some small rooms nearby for 'time-out' or small group work.

- You will only have what you have, but can you be creative? If you invest and get it right, the provision will support pupils for years to come and probably save the school a lot of money in the future. Find out how much the school is currently paying, or has paid, for alternative provision and add this to your case. **Cost vs benefit**.

As part of your strategic plan, you need to present detailed costs.

- How many pupils are you creating the provision for, as a maximum? This will dictate your staffing and your curriculum. I would advise to go for the same year group, or certainly the same Key Stage. Start small and allow it to grow. I would set a limit of about 12 pupils.
- What will your staffing model look like? You will need a lead and someone to deliver learning.
- What will your curriculum look like? Decide what you want to deliver and what can delivered based upon location/staffing/expertise.
- How will you support SEMH/behaviour needs? These children will come with challenges, so you need the right skill set for the staff. You can liaise with your SENDCO too, about any support they can give with staffing, or for them to teach in there as well.

This was the structure for our provision. The staff in the light grey boxes were expected to teach specific lessons.

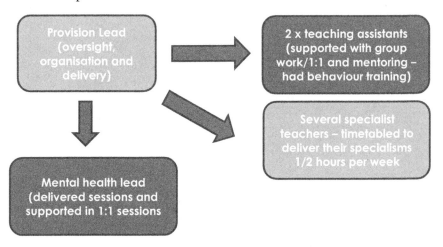

Curriculum offer

Remember the children who will access this will not have been able to access a full provision, so you need to look at their needs and then match that to your offer and your staffing. Deliver core subjects: you must not limit the Post-16 offer for these children. Then decide what the rest of their curriculum will be and do this with other leaders: the head, your outcomes lead, the head of year, the SENDCO. Make it a best-fit curriculum that supports the needs of the pupils and not necessarily the school. You will have to argue and drive this agenda strongly.

When setting up one of my previous provisions, we had spare staffing in English, geography and PE. We were able to match this to the skill set and qualifications of the provision lead and what they could deliver, and then we looked at the strengths of other departments and our facilities. The pupils ended up taking English, maths, science, geography and a fine art qualification, and this became our curriculum offer. We also timetabled some of the pupils to access mainstream classes, with support, where we knew they would succeed the majority of the time. Your teachers are the best asset you can have to ensure a child learns and gains qualifications, so it makes sense to use them when you can.

I cannot stress how valuable this type of provision is, but it does cost the school financially and it does have an impact on headline measures. My argument is the children accessing it need our support; they are our children and we need to help them. Another provision would cost more, may not fully support them and would also negatively impact on the budget and headline measures. **Cost vs benefit** again.

An internal alternative provision is such a powerful intervention to support your most vulnerable or challenging pupils, but it allows you to shape their future and for you to remain firmly in control of what their education looks like. If fully funded and run properly, you can positively impact children and families far more than using an external provider, and in the long term it will save you money.

Thinking point two

Reflecting on this information and your setting:

- What would be the biggest barriers in setting up a provision in your school?

- What do you think you already have in place that could work as a starting point?

Complete a SWOT analysis on your current setting – it could be the start of your strategic plan.

External provisions

Your school location will determine the alternative provisions on offer for your children. In larger Local Authorities, you will find a directory of the provisions you can access. It is worthwhile alongside this to link into the virtual schools that work with your children as they will be aware of specialist support. In smaller authorities you may have to research yourself, but no matter where you are located, don't forget to speak to colleagues in other schools – they may be using or know of excellent provisions.

Whatever is on offer, you have a duty to ensure that the provision is right for your pupils, and a visit and meeting with the provision leader is a must. Go and see it during the day and while children are there. It will give you a good feel and you can see what the learning looks like and what support they will get. Make sure, when you meet the leader, that you ask about safeguarding of pupils; get a copy of their policy too.

- Ask what the curriculum offer is and what other support may be available.
- Will children be able to access 1:1 support, a counsellor or some therapeutic work if appropriate?

It is up to you to assess whether the provision will meet the needs of your children. I would always take the child and their parents on a tour before making a decision so they can see the provision and be comfortable with it. Ensure they meet staff, meet other children and set up the chance for them to have a Q&A session at the provision.

Once you have agreed that you are going to use a provision, you must ensure you have all the details and be very rigorous with your safeguarding checks, making sure your service level agreements are tight and agreed upon. As DSL you will have oversight of all alternative provision, and you must know where children are and on what days/times. You will need to visit regularly and monitor their progress, support and safety.

What follows in Figures 8.1–8.4 are a few extracts of the document we use.

Service level agreement example

APPENDIX B

Alternative provision service legal agreement

The provider will ensure that they:

- Provide an agreed structured programme of learning, with clear aims, objectives and methods, leading to a nationally recognised qualification.
- Provide the Academy with their curriculum offer including details of all costings where possible.
- Provide all equipment and materials required.
- Provide a thorough induction programme, including health and safety, at the start of the programme.
- Carry out risk assessments, where appropriate, prior to the commencement of the programme.
- Provide a clear process for the reporting of accidents.
- Keep all student details in accordance with the Data Protection legislation and GDPR.
- Employ staff with relevant teaching and vocational experience and ensure their continued professional development.
- Collect and supply the necessary data for audit requirements.
- Contact the named person in the Academy immediately regarding any student whose behaviour or progress is causing concern. The Academy's permission must be obtained before sending a student off-site for any reason. Failure to do so will be considered as a breach of safeguarding protocols.
- Provide an identified person to be available for support.
- Monitor progress and provide half termly reports to the Academy and discuss the reports with the young learner at the end of each term.
- Record individual attendance and inform the Academy of absences daily.
- Maintain attendance record on site which can be inspected by at any time.
- Notify the Academy of any timetable changed or any variation.
- Comply with bullying and behaviour management guidelines.
- Comply with Academy's trips and visits guidelines and ensure that all necessary documentation is completed.
- Ensure that the Academy's child Safeguarding and Protection guidelines and policy are complied with.
- Ensure a designated safeguarding officer and an appropriately qualified first aider are available whenever students are on site.
- Ensure moderation and quality assurance systems are robust.
- Provide learning support for students who require it.
- Provide a free meal where there is an entitlement and have agreed lunchtime arrangements that are detailed in the student induction booklet.
- Invoice the Academy for the agreed amount on a termly basis

Figure 8.1

Checklist example

Checklist:

The following have been received and checked that they comply with the Academy's expectations

CHECKLIST	INITIAL/TICK
Health and Safety Policy	
Safeguarding Policy	
Risk Assessments .	
Personal Protective Equipment	
DBS Checks (& Included on Academies SCR	
Service Level Agreement	
Personal Education Plans	
Qualifications Offered	
Nominated Academy contact person	
Nominated AP contact person	
AP safeguarding lead person	
AP Student supervisor	

Figure 8.2

Parent/pupil agreement

APPENDIX D

Parent and Student Agreement

Name of student: Date of birth:

Information about Alternative Provision

Please find attached the referral form to enable your child (or the child that you have parental rights for) to take part in an alternative provision programme.

As the Academy have explained, alternative provision is a programme to offer your child the opportunity to gain work experience or gain other skills outside the Academy environment with carefully selected training providers.

The alternative provision provider will need to have access to certain information about your child, such as that contained in the referral form, to ensure that the programme offered and also any relevant pastoral support is appropriate to meet their needs.

The alternative provision provider will not disclose this information to any other party without express consent unless there is a legal requirement to do so or there is a risk of serious harm or threat to life.

All providers are required to ensure that health and safety and safeguarding requirements are met.

Please complete the following information:

Any medical or allergy conditions a provider would need to know about? Y/N

Emergency contact 1 name	
Telephone numbers	
Emergency contact 2 name	
Telephone numbers	

Figure 8.3

Safeguarding/progress/welfare checks

APPENDIX E

Progress Review Form 1

Student name:	
Alternative Provision name:	
Form completed by:	
Date of review:	

Attendance and Welfare 1

Cumulative attendance to date:	
Behaviour events	
Health and safety concerns:	
Safeguarding concerns:	
SEND interventions:	
Any agreed actions – record who, what and by when	

Progress 1

Predicted outcomes at last review:	
Predicted outcomes at this review:	
Interventions agreed	
Other outcomes/targets achieved since last review:	
Actions agreed (record who, what and by when):	

Figure 8.4

Specialist provisions

Accessing a specialist provision for a child can be the key that unlocks their door. It is really important that you start to work with these provisions, and use their expertise and skills. They specialise in key areas and you can form strong working practices. Formal access to them is through the EHCP route, and you need to evidence a thorough and detailed assessment of all interventions you have put in place. Your graduated response evidence is key here, as is the evidence your SENDCO will have from at least three cycles of Assess, Plan, Do, Review work.

Make sure you have clear evidence of work with educational psychologists, and that you have put in place their suggestions and can demonstrate impact. Once you have all this information, it can go to your Local Authority panel and an EHCP may be granted.

Whether a child has an EHCP or not, and whether a mainstream is named or not, you must really start to think about using specialist provision in some way. You could use a specialist setting and their skilled staff to offer therapeutic or clinical support for certain pupils. This kind of work helps the child understand how they feel and gives them the skills to deal with challenging situations they may face. You can disseminate these strategies with your own staff and allow the pupil to access a mainstream provision with in-class support.

There really are some superb external provisions out there. Think about how you can start to build working relationships with them. What can you offer each other?

One of the most powerful ways to work is through school-to-school support and use the knowledge, experience and skills of educational professionals. Link with these colleagues and think about how you can foster support work.

Can you give time to your staff to go and deliver in their provision and vice versa?

I have asked staff who work in a special setting to come and deliver CPD for our staff. We had several pupils who were finding school difficult, and specialist setting staff came along to observe and find a solution for us and the children.

As an inclusion lead in a school setting, I would always advise any leader to speak to Local Authority representatives and find out about their plans for allocation and spending of High Needs Block Funding. I have seen situations where not enough is spent on provision in the area and then the authority ends up spending a fortune educating children in specialist provisions outside their borough.

It is always worth a strategic chat about inclusive provision from time to time. Like in any job, the leaders in Local Authorities can easily forget what is happening and what is needed at the school level. Academisation and the development of trust provisions certainly don't help this, but I know you can get different multi-academy trusts, Local Authority schools and leaders together to plan for the right provision. I have been part of it. You just have to be brave and sometimes ask a difficult question. In the end it will be a yes or no, but at least there is a chance of a yes and a chance for children to get provision they deserve. I say, ask away!

Thinking point three

List the specialist provisions that you are aware of in your locality, without checking.

- How many are there?

- What do they specialise in?

- Do you already work with them?

Now research the provisions that are in your locality.

- How many more are there?

- Could some of them help your children?

Look at their websites and see what is on offer.

Leading inclusion scenario eight

Despite having a well-established package of pastoral support, year-on-year there are a small group of children who are not functioning in your school. They have repeat exclusions and despite the support on offer, they cannot seem to buy into school life. The governing body and trustees ask you as inclusion lead to draw up a plan that will support these children in Key Stage 4 and ensure that their exclusions reduce. Several colleagues are keen for these pupils to be sent elsewhere. You want to keep them in school and support their needs further with a bespoke provision.

Provide a paper that details a cost vs benefit analysis of using external provision against setting up one in school. The report needs to be written for governors and trustees, so think about the language you use and the argument that you formulate. Can you offer two or three actions for them to discuss and get back to you with?

It should be no longer than three pages and have key financial, curriculum, staffing and outcome data within it.

Use your own setting and any data, costings and staffing models that you can.

9 The children

This is probably the most important chapter in the book. This is why we do what we do, purely for the children.

The impact of 'behaviour'

In the role of leader of inclusion you will face daily challenges that can push your buttons and test your ability to be calm, patient and objective. Children will say or do things that beggar belief, and you may have witnessed or been subjected to verbal or even physical abuse. These are tough times, and they can have such a negative impact on you as a leader.

There is certainly no room for these types of behaviours, and it is your job to stamp these out and to educate children on what behaviours are acceptable. There are times in the job where you will have to make decisions that may impact negatively on a child and you have to show tough love in these situations. As a leader of inclusion, you cannot allow poor choices and poor behaviours to go unpunished or be deemed acceptable in society. Children need to learn that there are boundaries and there are ways of behaving that are just not okay.

Remember to use your policies and your systems, and you will set the bar. There are times when children have to be given a consequence for their actions. You also have to show the other children what is not acceptable and keep them safe from harmful behaviours. Remember your ethos and your values and reflect that the children may be trying to communicate something to you through their behaviour. In this job there is no better reward than supporting a child to improve their behaviour and the way they manage their emotions.

A big part of my ethos is to ensure that we generate positive experiences for children on a daily basis. A positive experience makes you feel so much better, and in turn influences how you behave and interact with others. Children need to be cared for: they need positivity, love and attention. This chapter is going to look at how we can develop the whole child. What experiences can we give them? What life lessons can they learn whilst in our care and how can we prepare them for the world?

Thinking point one

Think back to your time at school.

- What are your fondest memories? List them and at the side describe the feelings you have/had when (a) you were there and (b) when you remember them now.

- Finally, did you have any negative experiences? If so, detail how these affected you then and now.

Jot down your reflections.

Personal development and character

If I reflect on myself as a leader, on my morals, my values and my passion, I know these originated from my family and my upbringing, but also from my time in school. My experiences there and my relationships with other children and staff really did shape who I am today. If we are really going to develop our children, then we must pay sufficient attention to developing their character and developing them holistically.

How, as a leader of inclusion, can you ensure that your pupils get a wide variety of positive experiences? The term 'cultural capital' has been doing the rounds for a while now, and while I think it is such a strange term, it is directly linked to pupils' personal development, and as a leader you need to be thinking how you develop this.

Personal development is a big part of the new framework, so it would be very naïve not to pay this some attention and ensure it is evidenced throughout your work. There are already some excellent examples of experiences and 'promises' that have been developed and delivered by some of the larger trusts. As a leader of inclusion, can you develop a school promise or passport for your children and plan and deliver experiences through each year of their schooling?

I have broken down these 'experiences' into what I think are four key categories, and I have highlighted key aspects of each one and what you can do to set these up in your setting. This is what I call a Personal Development Portfolio.

The Personal Development Portfolio

If we are going to develop the whole child, then we need to be brave and not just focus on the **academic**. We need to offer experiences that develop a child's character. As educators, we need to ensure that we raise a child's **awareness** of the world and what is out there and available to them. Many children from disadvantaged backgrounds rarely get outside of their own town or area. We need to broaden horizons.

School should be a place to create lifelong memories, and we have so many opportunities to do this and take children on **adventures** that they can remember into their adult lives. Finally, we have to show an **appreciation** of our children, their lives, their community and for them as individuals.

Academic

No matter what community you serve, ensure that academic success changes lives. You must lead inclusion with a supportive focus, but you must also lead it to dovetail academic excellence. You must promote high expectations and give every pupil the best chance they have of success. This can be stamping out low-level disruption in class, letting teachers teach and then ranging to ensuring a child with SEND needs gets the support they need to succeed. Whichever way you support the children, academic excellence in our country opens doors.

It is your duty as a leader of inclusion to ensure you are aspirational in your mindset and your work – you have to have high expectations and strive for only the very best for ALL your pupils. In some communities, it can take considerable time to shift a mindset or alter aspirations. In these communities, it is your job to raise the bar even higher and flood your setting with success, ambition and positivity.

Make sure that you lead a pastoral culture of success and celebrate at each and every opportunity. Use assemblies, social media, postcards, phone calls, letters, display boards, weekly newsletters and so on. The more you celebrate success, the more your children become accustomed to it and will want it more.

Think about how you can influence them with positive role models. If you serve a disadvantaged community, your alumni base may not be too large. If you can, seek out ex-pupils who are now in a successful job or at university, and ask them to come and speak to groups of children. There is nothing more powerful than a speaker who is a member of the community. Children relate to them.

Allowing teachers to teach

Having been a leader in three different secondary settings, I can reflect on the most powerful tool you have to get academic success and raise aspirations: your teachers.

If your teachers do what they do best (teach, inspire, educate and build positive relationships), then you are a long way along the road to creating better life chances for your children. As a leader of inclusion, it is your job to do everything in your power to let your staff do what they do best. One of the most destructive things in a school is low-level disruption. Work hard with your pastoral team to stamp it out.

The systems that I talked about in Chapter 4 will help you. They will highlight areas of concern and they will show you patterns of poor behaviour. Empower your staff to have confidence to use your behaviour policy and to set a high bar around the expectations in the classroom.

Pair your behaviour system and classroom rules with effective consequences, and you will create a culture where learning is the priority and academic success will follow. I sometimes hear about pastoral colleagues undermining teaching staff by offering too much support or allowing a child to give excuses for poor behaviour. My advice to anybody who is leading inclusion is to never undermine them or their authority in front of the children. If you believe that a colleague hasn't followed the policy or their classroom management is poor, you need to have a conversation with them once the children have left. As a leader of inclusion, implement a simple, effective behaviour management policy that allows teachers to teach effectively and promote learning and success in the classroom.

Finally, work closely with your SLT colleagues and ensure that your curriculum model has an academic purpose but has the flexibility to meet the needs of your children. If you're going to meet the academic needs of every child, then you need an inclusive curriculum. Expose the children to a wide variety of subjects and ensure that there are opportunities for all. External accountability measures will always dictate part of our curriculum, but the new framework allows brave leaders to make brave decisions in the best interest of their children.

Academic excellence will come with a balanced curriculum, good teaching and developing children's experiences of the world. Make sure you have a work experience programme, and that you allow children to experience all there is to offer in further and higher education alongside the world of work. If you want academic excellence in any school or community that you serve, the children need to experience success, high aspiration and high expectations.

Awareness

In order to fully develop a child, we have to create opportunities to increase their awareness of what the world is like. In this day and age, it is so easy for a child to access a phone, a tablet or their computer to get a view of the world. The vast majority of information that children access via these devices is usually through social media. This can give a distorted, and sometimes prejudicial, view of the world.

It is our job as teachers to create awareness of what is right and what is wrong, and to give an impartial view so a child can make a decision themselves. Children who grow up in a disadvantaged community may have less opportunity to access different experiences. This limits their awareness of the world, of what they could achieve and what they ultimately aspire to be. It is part of your job to make a child's aspirations and ambitions limitless, and your pastoral and curriculum offer must reflect this.

As a leader of inclusion, shape the personal development opportunities that are on offer for children. They will gain experiences, knowledge and insight in the curriculum. A broad offer will subject them to different countries, places, cultures and religions. It will also give them knowledge of health, fitness, competition, famous people and events. Furthermore, it gives them the skills to draw, perform, play and debate. It is what you can offer outside of this time that can further enhance their awareness.

In all the schools I have worked at, we have always come together as a staff to celebrate events and to give children increased awareness of the world. Can you and your staff come together to plan events such as:

- Celebration days or taster days (other countries' culture/cuisine)
- World Book Day
- Pythagoras Day
- Remembrance Day events
- Holocaust Day remembrance

On these days, staff embraced the theme by dressing up and running different lessons and events throughout the day. Be creative and don't be afraid to do this. We need to offer breadth and variety from the exam factory direction that I feel we are forced down. One thing I know for sure: your staff will embrace it and be a key part of the journey.

Thinking point two

- What 'days' or experiences have you been part of as (1) a child in school or (2) a member of staff?
- Why were they successful or not?
- What days and experiences would you like to create in your current setting?
- How would you plan these?
- Who would you involve?
- What benefit would they bring to raising children's awareness?

Jot down your ideas.

Delivering the message

Work with your teams in your setting, and think about how you can raise awareness and deliver key messages within each subject area. Some year groups need different topics and themes. Think Internet awareness and safety for younger ones, and university life for Key Stage 4.

With your teams, think about the vehicles that you can use to deliver your themes, things like PSHE, assemblies, form time, visits and drop-down days. In some settings you will be responsible for the PSHE curriculum. Could you shape this so that you cover all of the key topics throughout the five years? Can you include topics that raise awareness of the world as well as the usual topics like health, friendships and sex?

Think about inviting guest speakers into school. Invite people from different walks of life and contrasting cultures to the community you serve.

Can you use live speakers to cover issues such as racism, homophobia, sexuality and so on?

The harder hitting, the better. There are some amazing companies out there doing amazing performances. Experiencing a live event will have more of an effect than a teacher delivering everything in a classroom setting.

Use your development plan to help you to strategically lead this and use your budget to pay for the costs. It is money well spent. On the back of these performances, pupils can use their experiences and motivation to form working groups and develop leadership opportunities, debating societies and drop-in support groups. The more experiences and awareness you bring to the children, the more you will perk their interest. For me this is a strategy that is really simple, but very powerful. The children love it and develop their awareness of some of the most challenging issues in society.

Adventures

Your extra-curricular offer is as important as your academic offer. A child's time in school should be exciting; it should be an adventure and we should be the facilitators of creating lifelong memories for our children. We have lost a bit of this in the past decade: the accountability, the outcome process and pressure on staff time have led to less adventures. I am passionate about ensuring that we create adventures and memories for children in school.

If I reflect back on my school experiences, they are filled with fun and happy memories – it was a challenge too, but trips to Alton Towers, to Spain on a water sports holiday, geography residentials, sponsored walks and countless sporting away day adventures outweigh the challenges. The impact of COVID, of domestic violence, of ACEs and a rise in SEMH needs will continue to hit our children hard. We have to start to think outside the box again and I firmly believe that adventurous experiences will help to negate some of these.

This model creates amazing opportunities for our staff, too. It impacts positively on their mental health and their way of life. As a leader of inclusion, drive your extra-curricular and personal development agenda hard. I don't want children to go to a school where they just experience lessons on exam technique and the pressure that comes with it. I want them to experience so much more.

You can make your offer a blank canvas, and as leader of inclusion you can have a huge influence over what experiences the children may have. One of the most rewarding adventures I have led was a Year 7 residential. We used it as a way to build relationships and confidence, and to take some children out of their comfort zone. We created cooking, camping, cleaning, abseiling, weaselling and walking experiences. We also made sure that EVERY child went on the trip whether they could afford it or not. It takes time, planning and effort to do these things, but every member of staff I approached was up for it. It comes back to your ethos and your culture. Get the right people on the bus with you.

Thinking point three

- What trips and excursions do you offer now?
- Are they the same each year?
- Do they need freshening up?
- What do the children think about them?
- Can you map together all you do as a school and evaluate your current offer?

As well as creating adventure experiences, can you also think of creating academic adventures too?

- What opportunities can you create where children can develop their academic skills, but it can still be an adventure?
- Can you link with colleagues in other departments? Will they be wanting to broaden horizons in their areas too.

Simple things like reading mentors in English, or a debating society and going to debate against other schools, can boost experiences and the skills of children. These experiences will develop leadership in your children. Children thrive on leadership opportunities and being responsible for something, and we certainly forget that at times in secondary school. Work with your pastoral leaders and develop roles such as form reps and house captains and make it purposeful. Let them have responsibility for their schooling. Give the time and effort it needs, and start to give your pupils more of a say in their school life and ask them what they want.

As leader of inclusion, can you develop a leadership structure within your teams? One of my first jobs as a principal will be to create a student senior leadership team that meets weekly and feeds directly into the senior leadership meetings. I want them to have an agenda, take minutes and look at writing a pupil version of the school improvement plan. I want them to plan how to improve pupil experiences and I want to give them a budget to spend too.

- Could you develop something similar?
- Do you have prefects? What is their role?
- Could they chair the student senior leadership team?
- Are the current leadership roles for pupils purposeful and valued?

Appreciation

Your culture as a leader of inclusion is key in this aspect of the portfolio. Children should be at the forefront of all you do, and your work should be geared around them: the school is run for the children. It is important that everyone in the school has an appreciation of all the things that support children and make them flourish. Your ethos should ensure that success is a staple part of a child's daily experience. The experiences the children get will determine how they feel and influence how they behave.

As a leader of inclusion, make sure you are the model of this approach and ensure that the staff reflect this in all they do, too. It is our job to look out for the children, to stretch them, to support them and to care for them. As a leader of inclusion, I work on the percentage that my work is balanced: 51% to 49% in favour of the children. I am their advocate, and in each decision I make I need to have their best interests at heart. Relationships are vital in securing an inclusive school where children trust the adults. My view on this is simple: relationships are absolutely crucial. These relationships are built over time by staff and pupils showing an appreciation of what they both need and can accomplish by working together.

Empower the staff to build positive relationships by developing relentless routines that are applied consistently and fairly. Show the children there are clear boundaries and clear expectations. Once you have these relationships, children and adults work together within a positive culture, and there is mutual trust and respect. These ingredients are what make a successful school.

By bringing staff and pupils together through adventures, awareness and academic rigour, you enable them to build an appreciation of each other, and a well-balanced and solidified respect. It is all of these things that really creates appreciation.

Community work

Another important aspect to consider is the community that you serve. You must ensure that the work you lead and complete has an appreciation of your community.

- Do you hold open days?
- Do you have parent forums?

Think about how you can create opportunities for children to put things back into their community. There is a wealth of experience, knowledge and positivity within your school's community. Source it, open up to it and it will further strengthen your inclusive approach.

- Can you organise days where the children help to pack shopping at the local Tesco?
- Can you organise charity days, where the children raise money for local charities and then present the money they've raised?

- Can you organise litter picking sessions or days where the children can work together to tidy up a certain area of the local community?

- Can the school be the central vehicle in organising a summer fete or summer fair? Can you also include local businesses in this?

The more you show children ways of appreciating their community, the more they will buy into it and the more the local community will understand the importance they play in developing their children. Teenagers get a bad reputation in local communities; can you help to change this opinion and show the community that they have young people to be proud of?

Thinking point four

- What community groups are set up in your local community?

- Do they use the school already?

- How can you influence their work and use them to help develop your ethos?

- Is there a member of SLT that has a community focus in your school?

- Can you join up with them? What can you both plan together, and can you link things to your house competition and have parents and businesses that are joined to houses?

Jot down your thoughts.

Monitoring children's mental health

You must ensure that your team and the wider staff have a full understanding children's mental health. This comes from a clear policy, a child-driven ethos and relentless training and culture shaping. Regularly lead CPD on managing behaviour, on safeguarding and on creating an ethos that puts the children first.

Make sure you use all the different tiers of support that you have in place. I mentioned this earlier in the book; your form tutors are the first port of call, and you have to establish a culture where staff value this role and take pride in it. They should be the colleagues who notice any differences in appearance or behaviour. They should be the colleagues who are regularly speaking to parents and relaying positive messages home.

Tracking mental health

I have used the relationships between a form tutor and their tutees to track mental health in their group. You can create a simple data sheet and ask staff to comment on their tutees in a range between 1 and 4. An example is as follows:

Aspect of SEMH	Description	Score
Friendships and socialising	Struggles to make friends and is often on their own in class and on the playground. Concerns about their friendships groups and/or lack of.	0
	Positive character. Has a wide circle of friends and is regularly seen socialising with others. Confident and well-spoken about issues that concern them or others.	4
Safe and healthy	Safeguarding concerns raised. Can present with neglect indicators. Frequently absent.	0
	Excellent attendance. Always smartly presented and positive about school and home life. No concerns from a safeguarding perspective.	4
Positive contribution to school	Very rarely stays after school. Does not show an interest in or attend extra-curricular activities. Does not participate in trips or excursions. Few house points or rewards received. Lack of engagement in assemblies, discussions, group tasks.	0
	Widely involved in extra-curriculars and enjoys doing a variety of clubs. Eager to attend trips and excursions, and has an active interest in school life in and out of the classroom.	4
Pleasing teachers	Frequently in detention. Lots of negative behaviour points accrued. Poor relationships with numerous staff. Lack of progress in most subjects.	0
	Lots of positive points and very few negative incidents. Few or no detentions, and progress indicates accelerated progress in multiple areas. Positive relationships with staff.	4

The tutors input this data every half term, and it can be collated and presented as shown in Figure 9.1, putting all pupils in the tutor group on one page.

This allows you and your team to review the strategic picture of mental health in a year group. You can discuss any low scores and cross reference whether they are already accessing support or not. This can ensure that no child slips through the net and it makes you plan interventions appropriately. From these meetings, you can then update graduated responses and refer children to either internal or external interventions. This information can be the catalyst for Early Help Assessments or as evidence for a referral to counselling, and to provide evidence for CAMHS work.

However you set up your monitoring, tracking and support mechanisms in school, make sure the systems are easy to use and give you data that is accessible and useful. The crucial part of your role is to ensure that every child, no matter

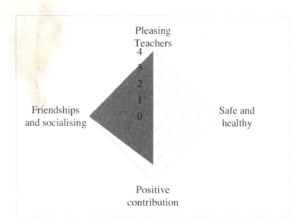

Figure 9.1

their ability, SEN status, age, background or other characteristics, can have success in your school. You are their advocate, their champion and ultimately the gate keeper to making their lives more stable and successful.

The leader of inclusion is one of the most important roles in a school setting. It is also the most challenging. Build your team, build your support and make sure you have systems that make your life easier.

It may be the most challenging role in a school, but it is the most rewarding and fulfilling position I could ever wish to have been in. I really do love my job and everything about it. I hope you grow to love the role equally as much.

Leading inclusion scenario nine

You are attending the monthly academic progress meeting with the head teacher, deputy head and each head of department. There are several pupils who have been identified across multiple subjects who are underachieving. You are aware of mitigating circumstances and external factors that could be some of the reason for this. You suggest moving the pupils out of a few lessons for some intensive work and even that some of them may not to be suited to the curriculum pathway they are on.

The deputy, who leads on outcomes, is not keen to remove children, as they feel this will further impact on their progress and it will have a negative impact on the school's figures. They are also against any subjects being dropped or movement away from the nine subjects they are studying.

You know that the lack of progress and engagement is down to external factors, and your ethos is to support children to succeed in whichever way is best. Think how you might contribute to the debate. How would you challenge the deputy? Should you? What evidence could you use? Is this meeting the correct setting for this? What might your next steps be?

10 OFSTED

This final chapter is designed to support the way you would present information prior to and during an inspection, and how you would lead a meeting with an OFSTED inspector or an external party. I will not go into how to address all aspects of the framework. This changes over time and I want this chapter to be relevant no matter what the framework is. As a leader of inclusion, it would be very naïve if you didn't prepare yourself for inspections, and ensure you follow the guidance and meet the requirements of the framework.

My OFSTED mantra is simple: do what is right for the children in your setting and have clear evidence and case studies detailing why. Most important of all though: '**fail to prepare, prepare to fail**'. Ensure that you have all the relevant data, documents and files ready to hand and prepared to discuss. This is where Chapter 4's systems are relevant and where your leadership of each topic in this book will dictate how prepared you are.

So how best can you do this?

Preparation

You will have a recent OFSTED report or, if you are a new or recently converted school, you will have some key areas of improvement. Make sure you have evidence that addresses any areas to improve; this is where the team will look first. If you haven't got a report, make sure you have the school development plan and then your impact evidence alongside. Make sure you are aware of any positive or negative factors you have aligned to key cohorts and key topics, e.g., pupil premium, attendance, SEND. If these figures are less favourable, then you need to demonstrate how you are addressing these and that you are aware of them. I have a Pastoral Report that I ask all our pastoral leaders to contribute to. This report contains the following:

- Pastoral development plan and all relevant quality assurance and strategic enabler documents as shown in Chapter 2.

- An overview of attendance – this is a printout of the tracker's headline figures and all key cohorts broken down. I then have an attendance report that compares internal data over the past three years that our attendance lead produces every half term. This includes attendance case studies, number of home visits, 90s club data, fines, letters and so on.

- An overview of exclusions – detail of numbers of fixed-term exclusions, broken down by year and key group, with a comparison to national data and the past three years. It also has a comparison to the number on roll, as this can be a good indicator. Again, I have case studies about repeat offenders and will use alternative provision documents to support my argument and to show the impact on repeat offenders.

- Behaviour data – but not too much. Show internal exclusions/detentions and so on, but don't shoot yourself in the foot. Make sure you balance it out with positive data and rewards too.

- A SEND report about the number of SEN registered pupils, number of EHCPs, and progress and attendance figures.

The key to all of this is to ensure you have the systems in place and the data to hand. The last thing you want to be doing after you get the call is spending hours trying to put packs together and finding data. By routinely using these systems, producing reports and constant quality assurance, once the call has come, the leaders in your team will just locate the reports and the data. Preparation and organisation are key.

On the morning of the inspection, I put all of this information into packs with clear headings and I leave them on the inspector's table. That way they can review them and dip in and out, and they don't have to keep coming to find you to ask for more.

Leading the meeting

Have no doubt in your mind, you will be asked to meet an inspector and go through key data, answering their questions. If you know your data and your areas of improvement, it is pretty easy to predict what the inspector's lines of enquiry will be. Just make sure that when you go into that meeting you have everything with you. I ensure that I take a couple of other key leaders with me, usually my attendance lead and another pastoral leader. Make sure you have rehearsed the meeting with them, but also empower them to contribute on their areas.

I have been involved in over ten inspections and I have led all the meetings. It is important that you go and show the inspector how you work as a team. Think of the following:

- Direct them to the paperwork and the figures.

- Control the direction of the meeting.

- Start strong and show your successes early.

- Show clear impact – especially if it is around one of their areas for improvement.

- Be confident and don't let them lead you. You own these systems and this area; show them how you do it.

- Be prepared for tough questions.

Inspections have changed. Inspectors will not spend hours dwelling on one thing, especially if you have the data and information to hand; show them you have it covered and move on. Always have in your head that an inspection team is always looking at how the leaders in the school lead and if they know what they are doing.

Starting the process

If you are the DSL, then you will without a doubt be the first port of call, and you can make or break an inspection based on this first interaction – no pressure there, then. The first meeting of the day will be the safeguarding one. Get any aspect of this wrong and the inspection will change direction and you could end up in special measures.

The first thing the inspector will want to see is the SCR, and they will ask to see a variety of staff's details, ranging from a cleaner to a governor. There are lots of flowcharts and checklists that tell you what you need to have in your SCR. Just make sure they are all there and there are NO GAPS. Those regular half-termly meetings with whoever inputs the data into your SCR are crucial – this is where you regularly check everything is in place. Make sure you have all the checks, and make sure that if you are an academy that you have done the leadership checks too.

This is where I lead the meeting again and I take the inspector down the safeguarding evidence path. I will show them documentation of staff CPD (with dates), Keeping Children Safe in Education evidence, staff safeguarding quizzes and details of staff who are safer recruitment trained. I will print off CPD sessions the team or I have run and show them.

Finally, I will have spreadsheet evidence of the following:

- Number of children on child protection/child in need/Early Help Assessment plans (and examples of reports we write).

- Number of referrals to social care with dates, names and the outcome – I will also add any escalations we have done, and I will direct the inspector to these.

- The number of referrals and outcomes from the LADO and any investigations I have led on.

- The number of children who have been on a partial timetable, with all the paperwork, the reviews and the justification.

- The number of pupils accessing alternative provision and every single alternative provision folder as we discussed in Chapter 8.

- The number of bullying/peer-on-peer abuse figures and any outcomes.

- Any meetings I have had with the safeguarding governor and any safeguarding audits.

The OFSTED framework

To finish the chapter, I am going to make reference to the framework. No matter what version is in place, I can guarantee that as leader of inclusion you will need to discuss leadership, behaviour systems, exclusions, attendance and safeguarding. There will be discussion around preparing the children for adulthood and being global citizens, so have evidence of personal development and PSHE work.

As the leader of inclusion who is reading this, you have to realise how important your role is to the success of school. Your work is entwined in every aspect of school life and, as you will see later in this chapter, your work will give clear justification of the outcome the school gets in an OFSTED inspection. It also shows the relevance and need for this book, for training and for the support that a leader of inclusion needs.

Leadership

The leadership of the school is judged on safeguarding. It is also judged on outcomes and how the leaders plan and make the necessary adjustments to ensure children at the school succeed. It is judged on the balance of the curriculum model and how leaders ensure this meets the needs of all children. The pastoral development plan and regular quality assurance highlight the value you bring to this process. If all the evidence discussed in this chapter is presented in a systematic and impactful way, the leader of inclusion is contributing to this judgement. The professional development of staff is vital to ensuring the school moves forward and that staff feels supported, entrusted and that they have a career pathway. Behaviour training, safeguarding training and consistent application of values and an ethos all contribute to this. Strategic leadership of SEND and how pupils with the most needs fare within the school setting is part of your work and add to this judgement.

Outcomes

The way children are supported and cared for is key to this strand. Work done by the leader of inclusion will impact directly on the outcomes of children. If children are going to succeed, they need to be attending school and to have any barriers lifted. The leader of inclusion will have oversight of pupil premium plans, and

Index

Note: Page numbers in *italics* indicate a figure on the corresponding page.

90 club 99, *99*

academic excellence 134–135
academic progress 73, 142
academic success 134–135
academisation 130
ACEs *see* adverse childhood experiences
adverse childhood experiences 44–45
alternative provision: benefits of 121; definition of 121; exclusions and 122, 131; external provisions 126–129; internal provision 123–126; specialist provisions 129–131
angling, as driver to change behaviour 115
assessment process 81–83
Assess, Plan, Do, Review (APDR) cycle 42
assistant head teacher 27, 29
assistant SENDCO 27, 39, 94
Athena 41–42
attainment: and attendance, correlation between 93; gap 107, 109, 115, 119; with teaching and learning model 116
Attainment Gap, The 107
attendance 93–95, *96*; data set 105, *105*; description in case studies 103, *104*; disadvantaged pupils 106; electronic tracking system for 102, *103*; encouragement strategies 98–100; key cohorts and groups 103–104, *105*; positive strategies 95, 97–98; and punctuality, OFSTED framework for 73, 101–102, 106; punitive strategies 100–101; pupil premium plan for improving 115; SEN data 102; tiered approach to 101; trust driver group/school-to-school support 105–106
audits 91
authenticity 15
awareness of world 133, 135–137, 139

behaviour management policy 49, 135
behaviour management systems: classroom rules 49–50, 135; consequence flowchart 50, *51*; developing 49–51; embedding 52–55; IT-based reporting mechanism 48; measuring impact of 58–62; middle leadership aspect 50; 'on-call' system 50; outcomes of: fixed-term exclusion 55–58; positive approaches 64–65; setting up and implementing 48; *see also* consequence tiers; detentions; reward system
behaviours 132–133
behaviour support workers 26, 94
Bridge, the 40
briefing 14

CAMHS *see* Child and Adolescent Mental Health Service

INSET – In-Service Training Day
ITT – Initial Teacher Training
LAC – Looked After Children
LADO – Local Authority Designated Officer
MLD – Moderate Learning Difficulty
NQT – Newly Qualified Teacher
PIL – Post-Incident Learning
PSHE – Personal, Social and Health Education
PSP – Pastoral Support Plan
SALT – Speech and Language Therapy
SEMH – Social, Emotional and Mental Health
SEN – Special Educational Need
SENDCO – Special Educational Needs Coordinator
SIP – School Improvement Plan
SLT – Senior Leadership Team
SMART – Specific, Measurable, Accepted, Realistic and Time-phased (reference to target setting)
SWAPP – Schools Wanting an Alternative Placement Panel (a term used and created by schools in Sheffield)
TA – Teaching Assistant
UPS – Upper Pay Scale – a zone on the Teachers' Pay Scale
WAGOLL – What A Good One Looks Like – reference to a teaching and learning strategy to model good practice

Glossary of terms

ACEs – Adverse Childhood Experiences – stressful events occurring in childhood including:

- Domestic violence
- Parental abandonment through separation or divorce
- A parent with a mental health condition
- Being the victim of abuse (physical, sexual and/or emotional)
- Being the victim of neglect (physical and emotional)
- A member of the household being in prison
- Growing up in a household in which there are adults experiencing alcohol and drug use problems

CEO – Chief Executive Officer
CPD – Continuous Professional Development
DSL/DDSL – Designated Safeguarding Lead/Deputy Designated Safeguarding Lead
EEF – Education Endowment Foundation (https://educationendowmentfoundation.org.uk)
EHA – Early Help Assessment
EHCP – Education, Health and Care Plan (previously a 'Statement of Special Educational Need')
EPEP – Electronic Personal Education Plan – these are used to design SMART targets and account for the spending of pupil premium money for LAC
GDPR – General Data Protection Regulation
HMI – Her Majesty's Inspector (with reference to a level of an OFSTED inspector)
HR – Human Resources
ILPs/IEPs – Individual Learning Plans/Individual Education Plans – strategies highlighted to support pupils on the SEND register as part of the Quality-First Teaching wave

how the school uses this money to improve outcomes for disadvantaged children and how they close the gap. The outcomes of children with SEND and how they compare to those without a need will impact this judgement and demonstrate the importance of this role.

Behaviour

All aspects of this are the result of strategic and operational leadership of a leader of inclusion: systems, processes, graduated responses, interventions, alternative provision, rewards, attendance, pastoral care and all the case studies that show the impact that a leader of inclusion has on families of the community.

Personal development

This aspect is evidenced through the work the leader of inclusion does with children on experiences, trips and visits. It can be evidenced through external speakers, external courses, assemblies and 'marks' the school can earn. The leader of inclusion can impact this area by actively developing pupil leadership and ensuring pupils have a voice. They can set up leadership opportunities that cover key topics and areas, such as LGBTQ+, anti-bullying and more.

I hope by referencing all of this you can see the importance of the role and why I feel it is one of the most important and impactful leadership roles in school. Of course, other leaders are key and all of the staff in school contribute to its success. Yet no other role has such a direct impact and influence on so many areas of a child's development.

The leader of inclusion in a secondary school is one of the most challenging and rewarding jobs in education. I hope this book has given you an insight to this and I hope it will help other leaders of the future to be successful and directly impact on the lives of children for the better.

centralised detentions 53
Child and Adolescent Mental Health Service 122, 141
child development 132; academic success 134–135; appreciation of community 139–140; awareness of world 135–137; delivery of message 136–137; extra-curricular offer 137–138; mental health monitoring 140–142; personal development and character 133; positive relationships, building 139; positive role models 134; *see also* SEND children
child protection 76–77, 81; *see also* SEND children
Children's Act 1989 81
children with SEND needs *see* SEND children
communication 14–15; importance of 13; needs of pupils 34; professional expectations of staff 33; with staff body about children 13
community: appreciation of 139–140; contribution 73; and ethos 4
consequence flowchart 50, *51*
consequence tiers 52
consolidating learning 118–119
continuous professional development 27
continuum of needs 79–80, *80*
counselling 45–46
CPD *see* continuous professional development
cultural capital 133
curriculum 123; content 45; inclusive 36, 135; led financial planning 36; models 36, 135, 146; offer 9, 41, 125–126

designated safeguarding lead 44, 84, 86, 91; attending child protection conferences 83; Early Help Assessment 81; investigation of disclosure 78; responses to assessment outcome 81–83; single central record and 86; team around family support 82; vigilant culture creation by 85
detentions 52–55, *55*
disadvantaged children *see* pupil premium
disclosure, reporting and managing 78
dramatherapy 45
drive 13
DSL *see* designated safeguarding lead

Early Help Assessments 44–45, 78, 81–82, 101, 141
education 50
Education Endowment Foundation: *Pupil Premium Guide* 107, 108–109, 115
education welfare officer 95, 101
EEF *see* Education Endowment Foundation
effective communicator 13–15
effective leadership 11
EHCP assessment 37, 42–43, 46, 129–130
Electronic Personal Education Plans 45
electronic systems 78
'eleos' 124
empathetic leadership 17
encouragement strategies, for excellent attendance 98–100, *99*, *100*
EPEPs *see* Electronic Personal Education Plans
ethos 3–6, 19, 31, 50, 132; and engagement 40–41, 124; for internal provision 124; reward system and 64
evidence 21, *25*, 37, 42–43, 97–98, 129, 141
exclusions and alternative provision 122, 131
external provisions 126–129; assessment of 127; checklist *128*; cost vs. benefit analysis of 131; meeting with leader of 126–127; parent/pupil agreement *128*; progress review checks *129*; safeguarding checks *129*; school location influence on 126; service level agreements 127, *127*; welfare checks *129*

face-to-face safeguarding training 87
Fair Funding Formula 108
Fantastic Friday 18
fixed-term exclusion 56, 58, 122
form tutors 26, 94
fundamental character 4
funding 108, 122, 144; for internal provision 123; for pupil premium 41, 107–108; for pupil premium plus 44, 45

GDPR *see* General Data Protection Regulations
General Data Protection Regulations 83
good teaching 26, 115, 119, 135
governor meeting 90
graduated response 37, 77, 108, 141; Athena 41–42; to attendance 101; Bridge 40; ethos and engagement 40–41; evidence 129; hub 39; REACH 39–40
graduated response sheet 37–39, *38*
graduation rewards 69; active global citizen *69*, *71*; areas 72–73; leader *70*, *72*; positive contribution *70*, *71*; skilled independent learner *70*, *72*

half termly pastoral review 14
heads of year 27, 94
High Needs Block Funding 130
hotspots 56
house events 18
house system: 65–67, *66–68*

IEP *see* individual education plan
ILP *see* individual learning plan
inclusion: key facets of 1; lead 27, 46, 94, 104, 124, 130; meaning of 1–2; staffing structure 26–29, 46, 94, 104, 124, 130; *see also* leader of inclusion; SEND children
inclusive curriculum 36, 135
individual education plan 35–36
individual learning plan 35–36
induction and training 86–90
influence 18–19
information delivery vehicles 14
information overload 14
INSET days, being creative with 18
internal exclusion 56–57
internal provision 123–126
interventions meeting 14, 39

J-List 59

knowledge: as leadership attributes 12; professional development and 87

LADO *see* local authority designated officer
language use, internal provision 124

leader of inclusion 1, 42–43, 73, 143, 146; appreciation of work 139–140; behaviour management and 132–133, 135, 147; core values of 8–9; extra-curricular agenda of 137; influence on school culture 7; moral purpose of 5, 6; role in staff well-being 7; shaping personal development 135, 137, 147; support to child 6; *see also* communication; leadership; leadership attributes; safeguarding
leadership 10; operational 21, 25; strategic 20–21; traits of 11–12; types of 11
leadership attributes: drive 13; effective communicator 13–15; empathetic leadership 17; influence over others 18–19; knowledge 12; people focused 15–18; reflective 15
learning barriers 109–110
Learning Rainforest, The (Sherrington) 36
Learning without Limits 33
Local Authority 42, 62, 78–81, 83, 95, 101, 130
local authority designated officer 84–85
'Lodge, The' 124
logical consequence 53
low-level disruption 134

mental health: issues in schools 8; monitoring 140–142
morality 5

nativity plays 18
natural consequences 52
new starter blog 14
'no-no behaviours' 58
nudge letters 99–100, *100*

OFSTED framework 3, 143; attendance and punctuality 101–102, 106; attendance reference in 95; behaviour 147; leadership 146; outcomes of children 146–147; pastoral development plan and 21, *22–24*; personal development 147; school improvement plans and 20
OFSTED inspection 143–146
'on-call' system 50
one-page improvement plans 21, *22–24*
operational leadership 21, 25
operational safeguarding 77

parent/pupil agreement *128*
parking systems 56
pastoral culture 2, 134
pastoral development plan 21, *22–24*, 64, 95, 143, 146
pastoral support plan 59, 61, 62
pastoral team 10, 26–28, 69, 76, 95, 123
people focused leadership attribute 15–18
permanent exclusions 122
personal development portfolio 133–134
PIL *see* post-incident learning
poor behaviour 37; fixed-term exclusion for 58; incidents of 6, 121, 132
positive experiences 95, 132–133
positive role models 134
positive strategies, for excellent attendance 95, 97–98
positive work-life balance 7
post-incident learning 53–55, *55*
professional development 34, 87–90, 146
PSP *see* pastoral support plan
punitive strategies, for excellent attendance 100–101
pupil premium: barriers to learning for 109–110; criteria to be classed as 107; funding for 107, 108; good teaching *vs.* poor teaching for 115; progress in core subject areas 119; strategies for 110; work, statement about 116
Pupil Premium Champion 119
Pupil Premium Guide 108
pupil premium plan: angling as driver to change behaviour 115; barriers to learning 111, *112*; budget and spending 113–114, *113–114*; desired outcomes of *112*, 112–113; examples of 110–111, *111*; OFSTED requirement for 110; staff expertise and drive for 114
Pupil Referral Unit 121

quality assurance 61, 146; audits 91; governor meeting 90; and monitoring 97; random visitor 90; safeguarding team meeting 90
quality-first teaching 108; case study of 34–35; one-page profiles for 35–36; supporting provision of 34; 'teach to top' 36–37

Raising Engagement Attainment Communication and Health 39–40
random visitor 90
REACH *see* Raising Engagement Attainment Communication and Health
reflecting and reflection 15
remove rooms 55–56
resilience 37
responsive relationships 45
reward system 63–74; 'empowering positive' 64–65; factors influencing design of 63–64; graduation landing page 73–74; importance of 63; planning 64; strategic enabler evidence form for *25*; targets for 64; *see also* graduation rewards; house system

safeguarding: actions 75–76; board 79–80, *80*; checks, external provisions *129*; and child protection 76; concern with poor attendance 93; culture 84, 85, 86–90; definition of 75; as everyone's business 76–77; information 76–78; lead 27, 94; leadership strategy for 76; operational 77; partnership 78, 81, 83, 91; quality assurance 90–91; session 87; staff survey *88–89*; strategic 85; team meeting 90
school improvement plans 20, 95
school(s): culture 5–9; leaders 31
Schools Wanting Alternative Placement Panel 60–62; aims and purpose of 60–61; practice 61–62; quality assurance 61
school-to-school support 105–106, 130
SCR *see* single central record
section 47 assessment 82–83
section 128 check 86
SEMH needs *see* social, emotional and mental health (SEMH) difficulties
SEN Code of Practice 2014 30–33
SEND children 1, 46, 82; categories of 31, 32; consistent lesson cycle for 37; expectation of educational provisions for 31; failure to support 32; inclusion graduated response to 37–39, *38*; one-page profiles for 35–36; SEN Code of Practice 2014 30–33; strategic model for

33; substantial challenges 122; *see also* child development; child protection
SENDCO 28, 35–36, 39, 42–43, 94–95, 122
senior leadership team 15, 18, 87, 119, 138
service level agreements 127, *127*
single central record 85–86
SIPs *see* school improvement plans
SLT *see* senior leadership team
social, emotional and mental health (SEMH) difficulties: adverse childhood experiences 44–45; counselling 45–46; dramatherapy 45; mental health monitoring 141–142; support 43–44; symptoms and responses 44; trauma 43
social, emotional and mental health (SEMH) support 39
social services, referral to 78–79, 81
specialist provisions 129–131
staff, school: allegations against 83–84; inclusion structure 26–28; internal provision 125–126; involvement in system design 49; model behaviour 50; pre-appointment checks, database of 85–86; professional development of 146; well-being 7–8, 17–18
staff-specific requests 18
strategic enabler evidence form *25*

strategic leadership 20–21, 33
strategic safeguarding 85
subliminal messages 85
Sutton Trust 115
SWAPP *see* Schools Wanting Alternative Placement Panel
system, definition of 49

teaching and learning model 115, 117–119
'Teaching Walkthrus' 37
team ethos 5–6
thresholds: development of 78; four-tiered 79, 81; referral for evidence against 81
tiered consequences *see* consequence tiers
toxic stress 44
trauma 43–44
trust approach 49
trust driver group/school-to-school support 105–106

virtual schools 126
Vulnerable Learner Network 14

weekly staff briefing 14
welfare checks, external provisions *129*
well-being group 18
work experience programme 135